# HOW I SOLD A MILLION DOLLARS

# OF REAL ESTATE IN ONE YEAR

# HOW I SOLD
## A MILLION DOLLARS
## OF REAL ESTATE
## IN ONE YEAR

**George H. Gardiner**

**PRENTICE-HALL, INC.**          **Englewood Cliffs, N.J.**

PRENTICE-HALL INTERNATIONAL, INC., *London*
PRENTICE-HALL OF AUSTRALIA, PTY, LTD., *Sydney*
PRENTICE-HALL OF CANADA, LTD., *Toronto*
PRENTICE-HALL OF INDIA PRIVATE, LTD., *New Delhi*
PRENTICE-HALL OF JAPAN, INC., *Tokyo*

LIBRARY OF CONGRESS
CATALOG CARD NUMBER: 78–81316

PRINTED IN THE UNITED STATES OF AMERICA
13–399808–8    B & P

With immeasurable affection

this book is dedicated to Pimbo, Clownie and Mary Jane

and to those that love them.

---

The author gratefully acknowledges the invaluable assistance of Margaret Chenery Carmichael, without whose encouragement, editing, and technical direction this book would surely never have been written.

# CONTENTS

## 8. HOW I CORRECTED MY BIGGEST MISTAKE (Continued)

## 9. FIVE MAJOR MISTAKES THAT LOSE SALES . . . . . . 70

## 10. TWO SIMPLE FORMULAS THAT WORK LIKE MAGIC . . . . 86

## 11. THE ADVANTAGES OF BOW-AND-ARROW OVER SHOTGUN SELLING . . . . . . . . . . . . . . . . . 93

## 12. FIFTEEN MINUTES' OVERTIME GAVE ME THREE SALES IN ONE DAY . . . . . . . . . . . . . . . . . 109

HOW I SOLD A MILLION DOLLARS

OF REAL ESTATE IN ONE YEAR

# CHAPTER 1

# FROM FAILURE TO MASTER SALESMAN IN TWO YEARS

Sell a MILLION DOLLARS worth of real estate in one year? INCREDIBLE! When I first entered the real estate business such a thought would have been preposterous.

I was a nervous greenhorn salesman who stumbled over the pronunciation of his own name. At that time to earn even $10,000 a year was just a dream. As the months went by I learned that $10,000 a year was considered barely an average income in the real estate business.

Soon, however, I made the galvanizing discovery that the field of real estate is studded with HILLS OF GOLD! If I were to reach this wealth I would have to open some doors, but to do this I first had to find the keys—keys in the form of short-cuts, techniques, methods, secrets and even magic formulas.

And find them I did. The result was that in one year I SOLD ONE MILLION DOLLARS IN RESIDENTIAL REAL ESTATE!

## TRIED AND PROVEN METHODS THAT WON'T ALLOW YOU TO FAIL!

The purpose of this book is TO HAND THESE KEYS TO YOU. The hills of gold are still there—take the keys and help yourself. It's as simple as that!

Among the many amazing things about these magic keys is that

1

they work so easily. They open doors not only to a much greater income, but also to prestige in your profession, prominence in the community, and more material possessions to enjoy. In short, to a place at the banquet of success. These methods and techniques representing the keys are so simple and easily mastered that if you will adopt them you cannot fail, even if you try! I will show you how and why each one works and, in most cases, give you a step-by-step formula to practice. The application I will demonstrate by relating actual sales using each one, until all the techniques are covered.

I am thoroughly convinced that if you will follow these directions in their entirety, you, too, will sell ONE MILLION DOLLARS worth of real estate any year you choose to. Many of the techniques are unique, a few are borrowed and modified, but all of them I used to achieve my million dollar year.

## WORKING HARD AT FAILURE

However, this was not always so. The first few months, in the real estate business, goodness knows, I tried. I never worked so hard in my life but I couldn't make a nickel. Nothing would jell. Sales were being made all around me, I was working in a fine office in the suburbs of Chicago, the market was good—I should have been going great guns. But I couldn't beg, buy, borrow or steal a sale.

One day I overheard the owner of the business tell the sales manager that I would never make a real estate salesman.

I went home each night a sorry sight—a perfect picture of failure—a salesman who couldn't sell. I lacked five dollars of having a quarter; the house payment was overdue; I had a gasoline bill for more than my car was worth. I was very, very close to quitting the real estate business.

One night I poured out my sad story to a friend of mine, and concluded my tale of woe by asking him what he would do.

His answer was simple: "*I* would keep trying."

It would be nice to say that I went back to the office, made a sale and was on my way to success, but it didn't happen that way. I *did* go back, though, and once again threw myself into my work. I studied listings, I made phone calls, and whenever I could get my hands on a prospect, I ran him ragged. I worked with frantic determination, but the days went by and I hadn't even come close to a sale.

The time stretched into weeks, and I wondered why the ax didn't fall. Every morning when I walked into the office I expected someone else to be sitting at my desk. Finally I couldn't stand it any longer. I did what I should have done long before. I went to an old-timer in the office and asked him,

"What is wrong with me? Why can't I make a sale?"

His answer may be why I am still in the real estate business today.

## IN MATTERS OF SALESMANSHIP I HAD MISSED THE BOAT

"Your trouble is, you don't know what you're doing. You first must learn the techniques of salesmanship. You should read everything you can find about the real estate business. You sell real estate with your head, not your feet. Take the time to develop some methods and techniques: until you do, you'll just be spinning your wheels."

I eventually sold my first house and then another and finally settled into the role of a real estate man with an average income. The months rolled by and my income fluctuated from average to below.

For some time, however, I had been aware of a select group of real estate people in the area who were earning large commissions, winning awards, driving Cadillacs, and taking winter cruises in the Caribbean. I assumed they had something special going for them: that their education, social standing, or some such thing created a barrier that it was unthinkable for me to cross. I watched them from a distance with awe and envy.

Finally I began to feel a stir of discontent with my status as an average salesman, but still it smoldered under a cover of complacency for quite a time. Then one night, while I was attending one of many real estate seminars, it burst into a roaring flame. I heard a speaker who was just right for *me*. I don't remember his name, but what he said was intensely inspirational.

### THE ROUSING SPEECH THAT GOT ME GOING

His advice was, "Have the courage to develop NEW techniques. Have the audacity to experiment with old methods. If you're not getting results with the standard rules of selling, then discard them and write your own. But above all, don't be satisfied to exist in the gray world of mediocrity!"

This man was talking to *me*! What he said hit me where I lived. His words were the spark that kindled the intense excitement and enthusiasm about selling real estate that still burns in me today.

He concluded his talk that night by saying, "If you really intend to do something about improving your career, start tomorrow morning. If you don't, you never will!"

Those words completely changed my life, because I took his advice and the next morning started plotting a new career for myself. I began to experiment, to develop the techniques and methods and selling secrets that in an amazingly short time brought me a million dollars worth of sales in one year. I am going to explain and demonstrate them to you.

### A REVIEW OF THE REMARKABLE SELLING METHODS TO BE COVERED

Chapter 2 lists the major selling formulas that launched me on my biggest year. These include the theory of SELLING PEOPLE TO HOUSES RATHER THAN HOUSES TO PEOPLE, how to guide prospects to SELL THEMSELVES, how to bring out the clue that will make the sale BEFORE YOU LEAVE THE OFFICE, the TEMPERING TECHNIQUE, the decisiveness of the SHORT SPEECH, the SILENCE TECHNIQUE, and others.

A broader and more intimate study of the techniques listed in Chapter 2 begins with Chapter 3. Also in Chapter 3 the first of almost magical results from these adventurous techniques begin to appear.

The REVERSE SELLING and CHAIN OF QUESTIONS formulas that you will probably want to adopt immediately to add impetus to your career are explained and demonstrated in Chapter 4, along with the "DIRECT AND CONTROL" method and the use of the SI-LENCE TECHNIQUE.

All sales start with the listing, but all listings do not end in a sale. Chapter 5 explains how to take a listing and when to take it as well as when not to take it. Working with the TOP 10 PERCENT of the listings will help make you rich. This chapter tells how to accomplish that. The three steps that cover moving a listing into the top 10 percent conclude the chapter.

The decision-making forcefulness of the short speech is exhibited and demonstrated in Chapter 6. The HIDDEN QUALIFICATION and how to uncover it is also explained, as well as the sales-making power of the SHAKEDOWN TECHNIQUE.

Chapter 7 demonstrates the use of CONTROLLED ANGER. Some mistakes and their deadly effect on sales are revealed in Chapter 8 as well as the Positive Selling Attitude on the one hand, and the Negative Selling Attitude on the other.

Five specific major mistakes and how to correct them, with the incredible sales-producing results is the topic of Chapter 9.

How to be a magician in the real estate field is the theme of Chapter 10. Two formulas that work like magic, one that changes a renter into a buyer, and one that can be adapted to handle ANY PROBLEM of ANY KIND at ANY TIME!

A TARGET HOME, as the result of a keen qualification period and a PROBING FOR CLUES is referred to in the BOW AND ARROW method in contrast to the time-wasting amateurish SHOTGUN method, whereby a number of homes are tossed at a buyer in hopes he will buy one. Chapter 11 describes these methods. How to select a target home and how to force the KEY CLUE are the highlights of this chapter.

Chapter 12 attempts to demonstrate dramatically that you are in the real estate business 24 hours a day. The after-hours time spent at the office which led to a chain of three sales is a convincing example that although the hours are long, the pay is excellent.

"CREATING A CRISIS" is the delicate but powerful technique discussed in Chapter 13. It practically eliminates the "I want to think it over" prospect and will make you many, many sales heretofore lost. The THIRD PERSON ENDORSEMENT and the TRUTH AND TENDERNESS technique will further ease and simplify your task of making a sale.

SELLING THE SELLER is covered in detail in Chapter 14. You are shown how to maneuver the seller into his last stand, by convincing him that if he refuses your offer (assuming it is a fair one) he becomes a real estate speculator, and the folly of doing so.

Chapter 15 describes the simplified handling of the complex problems involved in a chain of fourteen sales; also, the story of the single act of kindness that brought about the fourteen sales.

How anger allowed to run rampant, and feelings that are easily hurt can put you right out of the real estate business, and what to do about it is the theme of Chapter 16.

Chapter 17 is filled with the romance of selling real estate. It is the story of the LILAC BUSH that was sold for THIRTY THOUSAND DOLLARS, and a STAINED GLASS WINDOW that brought TWENTY-FOUR THOUSAND DOLLARS. Proof that people buy with their hearts and not their heads is supported by the story of the DIAMOND RING, the THREE-CAR FAMILY, the GOLDEN BATH, and others.

How to increase your bank account from your competitors' mistakes is told in Chapter 18.

Chapter 19 tells how to harvest the profits made from sales passed up by other real estate people. Three overlooked sources for easy sales is the chapter title and it holds a world of profitable information.

The long story of the short-term exclusive is covered from every angle in Chapter 20.

Careful consideration before answering a calculated question brought me the LARGEST SALE OF THE YEAR. The step-by-step story of this exciting sale is told in Chapter 21.

You MUST be remembered to receive referrals and you MUST receive referrals to succeed. The many ways you can be sure you are remembered are discussed in Chapter 22.

Once you have been permeated to the core with all the methods and techniques of selling real estate, most of which we have just covered, you will want to slip into the mental automation, a computer of the mind, so to speak, which, now that you have programmed it, will handle with efficiency and alacrity the task of selling real estate while you are busy with other matters. This phenomenon is discussed in Chapter 23 under "INSTANT RECALL" and REM (Real Estate Memory).

These unique methods and techniques, astonishing in their simplicity, are tried and proven. I will show you what they are and how to use them by describing the sales and the methods that I used to make them during the year I sold one million dollars of residential real estate. This book is the story of that unforgettable year.

The outstanding lesson I learned during that year was the value of referrals. I firmly believe that with them you cannot fail: without them, you cannot succeed. You will receive referrals in direct ratio to your reputation as a real estate man.

Anyone in the real estate profession can sell a home. I believe that I enjoyed a somewhat greater success because of one small factor. Each time I sold a home, I saw to it that a small part of me went with it.

I will be highly gratified if the methods and techniques suggested here enable you to serve better what I think is the finest profession on earth: the marketing of real estate. You are the third party selling FOR the first party, TO the second party, for the MUTUAL BENEFIT of all three. Do IT WELL.

# CHAPTER 2

# THE EIGHT-POINT FORMULA
# THAT STARTED ME ON MY
# FIRST MILLION DOLLAR YEAR

---

The first secret was not a secret at all; rather, a simple deduction that to make more money I had to make more sales. It must be recognized that the number of sales necessary to generate a high income makes it mandatory that the selling time for each individual sale be reduced. Therefore, the specific selling secrets must produce a sale *in far less than the usual time.*

### A revealing deduction concerning the use of time

I had to continue making the regular sales that any average salesman makes—the type where buyers are looking for a standard house. They come to the office, look at a number of homes in their category and eventually buy one. This kind of selling will keep a real estate man in the average income bracket. It will also require 75 percent of his time, for a great amount of his time is taken up with waiting for buyers. It's a simple deduction to realize that to double his income he will have to make an equal number of sales in the remaining 25 percent of his time, and to triple his income he must make twice as many sales in the remaining 25 percent of his time. To accomplish the million dollar year I had to apply methods that would shorten the time necessary to produce the average sale, and would also create other sales. The key techniques I developed work like magic to accomplish these two most vital ingredients to selling success—speed and quantity.

## I WORKED EXCLUSIVELY WITH
## THE CREAM OF THE LISTINGS

I gained a great amount of *extra time* by concerning myself only with two or three of the best properties in each price class.

## I STARTED SELLING PEOPLE TO HOUSES,
## NOT HOUSES TO PEOPLE

Since I was handling the best listings, I needed only to convince my prospects of this and I usually had a sale. As I applied my newly discovered techniques, I found that 80 percent of the time I made a sale the first time out. Incidentally, it is my opinion that if you don't make the sale the first day you are with your prospects, the chances that you will ever sell them drop 50 percent. Assuming that you have qualified your prospect, and he actually is a buyer, it follows that he can be sold the best property there is on the market in his price range. Handling the problem buyer, or the buyer with unusual requirements, a fact, incidentally, that you should determine during the qualifying interview, will be explained in subsequent chapters.

## I LET MY PROSPECTS SELL THEMSELVES, OR
## THE "DIRECT AND CONTROL" METHOD

This is an easy, but delicate method, which will require a little practice, but once mastered, it works miraculously. The technique breaks into two parts. Reassured by the knowledge that I was handling only the best properties, I let the buyer sell himself by reversing the usual selling technique:

(1) While I was showing the property, rather than pointing out the good features of the house, I was a fault-finder, questioned quality, became critical. I was amazed to find that the buyers began to defend the house they were inspecting. Once the momentum

started, it always accelerated to the point that the buyers were literally selling the house to me.

(2) The technique in the second half of this method I call the chain-of-questions formula. It consists of a continual flow of questions, the nature of which forced the purchaser to answer affirmatively all of the questions I asked. I used carefully prepared questions, of course. If the questions were planned in the proper sequence, by the conclusion of the inspection I found that the prospect had sold himself. The question formula rated very high on the success scale, and I frequently alternated it with the fault-finding method described above. You may choose to use either method, but I assure you that both parts of this system accounted for many of the *extra* sales consummated during my million-dollar year. They hastened the decision to buy, freeing me to go on to the next prospects.

### I SEARCHED FOR TIP-OFF CLUES

I discovered that nearly all prospects, if I kept them talking, would almost invariably give me a clue to the property that they were most likely to buy. This explains, partially, why many of my buyers bought the first house I showed them.

These invaluable, time-saving clues fall into two categories:

*The unexpected clue.* Statements regarding the buyers' hobbies, financial status, background, social activities, personal peculiarities, general likes and dislikes frequently furnished me with the clue I needed for a quick sale.

I once spent an entire afternoon showing a young couple properties that I thought would produce a sale. I had given up and was returning with them to the office when the wife said, "This evening we're putting the second coat of varnish on an Early American dining set that we're going to use in our new home." There was the clue. They were buyers for an Early American type home, not the modern style we had been looking at. I acted on it and a sale was made that evening.

*The forced clue.* I controlled the conversation so that my prospects were not aware of what I was trying to do: otherwise they would give guarded answers. Giving false answers is the prospects' sales defense. Indicating my general interest, I led my prospects to talk about other homes they had occupied, other cities where they had lived, the type and location of the house they had been raised in, and homes of friends and relatives where they had visited, dwelling on each topic to see if I could bring out a clue to the house most likely to fulfill their true desires. Often the points uppermost in their minds were the result of suggestions and advice from friends, which momentarily submerged their true desires.

### The "inner person" furnishes the clue to the sale

I had high hopes of making a sale to one woman, but they diminished rapidly as the afternoon wore on. Like many buyers, she indicated she wanted one type of home, when in reality she wanted another. I guided the conversation to houses which had appealed to her in the past, and she described to me with great emotion the home of her aunt, which she had loved as a young girl. She dwelt on a description of a large dining room with a built-in, three-cornered china cabinet. There was my clue. I had such a house and a quick sale was made.

I found that, rather than trying to force a sale, which is extremely difficult, searching for and watching for clues reduced the selling time considerably. Always make it easy for a prospect to buy!

### THE TEMPERING TECHNIQUE

This produces excellent results with buyers who are indecisive. All buyers fall into one of the following categories: those who

1. Need a larger home
2. Need a smaller home
3. Want a better home because of increased income
4. Need a less expensive home because of decreased income
5. Are moving into the community
6. Are buying their first home
7. Buy for income purposes

I adapted the technique according to the type of buyer I had. It is not applicable, however, to the person who buys for income purposes.

### Why you must first sell yourself

For the tempering technique to be successful, I first had to set the stage. This required that during early association with my prospects, I made them emphatically and conclusively aware of my knowledge, not only of real estate in general, but of all the services and facilities in the community, and of the current terms of the various types of mortgages. I also proved that I had an above-average knowledge of home construction and, particularly, of current market values. If I could convince the buyer that he was in the hands of an expert, he would relax, listen respectfully, and be receptive to my advice. I found, however, that using this technique produced little success unless I had set the stage well.

### Stalled prospects who need a pointed prodding

Unlike other methods discussed, careful timing is essential with the tempering technique. I used it almost as a last resort. When I had reached the point where I realized that I had done my job, but the prospects hadn't done theirs, I knew it was time for the tempering technique. I had shown them the very property they wanted to own; they knew it, and I knew it. I had convinced them the intrinsic values were greater than the cost. However, they were unwilling to admit that they wanted to buy it. They were secretly hoping for a house just a little better or for one at a little lower price.

### Insist upon their undivided attention

I would wait for an appropriate time, if the prospects were in the car with me. I would seek a quiet street, for there must be no distractions, and, without explanation, pull over to the curb, shut off the ignition and turn to face my prospects. With a serious look and a stern tone, I would say, "It's time we had a heart-to-heart talk. I want you to listen to me very carefully. . . ."

### The short speech

With just enough heat in my words to temper their unjustified indecisiveness I would point out the facts. I would tell them I had done my job; I had found them a good house at a good price, that suited their needs and desires, and for them to procrastinate, hoping for something a little better, was foolish, wishful thinking. I would explain the inadvisability of their attitude and why it would ulti-mately result in their making a bad buy. I would continue with this line of reasoning, gently rebuking them for being impractical, until I sensed that they understood and agreed. From then on I was in control and the problems disappeared. If it was done carefully and conscientiously, I found this technique almost sure-fire.

### THE SILENCE TECHNIQUE

This requires self-control and good acting ability, and a top salesman should have both these traits.

When you have determined that you have shown a property to your prospects that fills all their needs and desires, and they are fighting you as you attempt to close, apply the silence technique.

In the privacy of your office or their home, get their full atten-tion, restate all the reasons why this house fills their needs and desires, then say to them, "Now, Mr. and Mrs. Buyer, let me ask you a question: Is there *really* any reason why you shouldn't buy this house RIGHT NOW?" Then stop. Don't say another word. Transfix them with your eyes and let the silence do your selling. As the seconds tick away they will fidget and squirm until it becomes almost unbearable for them. If they break the silence with a state-ment or question, handle it, then again put the silence to work. Say to them, "Let me ask you again: Why don't you buy this house NOW!" And wait. You'll get your sale.

### WHAT BECOMING A SPECIALIST
### WILL DO TO YOUR INCOME

Becoming a SPECIALIST should double your income. Applying the techniques of selling described in later chapters should double it *again*.

Today's world is a world of specialists, and in real estate you have a broad field out of which to choose your specialty. In this book we are discussing primarily how to sell residential real estate and, although the field is limited, it does have various categories. A list would include:

1. Low-priced homes ($12,000 and under).
2. Homes for the middle-income buyer.
3. Small income property with resident owners; mobile home courts; business property with residence included.
4. Farms, ranches, and suburban homes.
5. The unique, the unusual, and the expensive homes.

You may take your pick, but whichever one it may be, your sales will soar if you truly become a SPECIALIST. One of the surprising results is that even competitors will occasionally send you a client.

### A one-street specialist

I once knew a real estate man who could be called a "strip" salesman. He specialized in ONE STREET. It was a main artery comprised almost entirely of business property, and with the help of a strip map and the courthouse records, he kept track of each property, with the owner's name and address, and whether or not it was for sale or lease. He noted every sale that was made, the price, the new owners, and their intended use of the property. He was a SPECIALIST and for many years enjoyed a high income from the sale and resale of the property on this ONE street.

### Specialists are sought out first

So be a SPECIALIST. This does not mean, of course, that you cannot venture into the other real estate fields when the opportunity arises, but it does mean that you will make the majority of sales in your chosen field of specialization, because *you* will be the expert that others will turn to when action is desired. In almost any field of endeavor today it is the specialists who survive and enjoy the highest incomes. The incredible amount of real estate that changes hands every day has made obsolete, for all intents and purposes, the one-man office or the salesman who generalizes rather than specializes.

When I chose the last category on the list above, things started to happen. It was a matter of selecting the unique, unusual, and expensive homes that I personally wanted to handle. Next I had to become thoroughly and intimately acquainted with every detail and fact about them and their owners. Finally, it was necessary to develop techniques specifically tailored for use in this category.

The decision to specialize in one area of residential real estate was the major factor in my reaching the ONE MILLION DOLLAR figure in sales in ONE YEAR.

## ASK THEM!

This is so simple a matter, but many and many a sale has been lost because of it. When buyers showed interest in a certain house the salesman neglected to ask them point blank, "Would you like to buy this house?" So ASK THEM!

These are the major techniques that accounted for most of my extra sales during the million dollar year. These techniques and other methods, will be amplified as they are demonstrated in particular sales described in later chapters.

CHAPTER 3

# A SIMPLE DISCOVERY THAT DOUBLED MY INCOME

As I took an objective look at the methods being used to sell real estate I was literally amazed at the manifold efforts being put forth daily by those involved in its marketing.

There were hundreds of properties on the market, each with its own features and selling points, waiting to be sold. There were also a great number of buyers, each with his demands and peculiarities, searching for a home to purchase. The seemingly hopeless task of matching the right buyer with the right house faces the real estate man each day.

I felt much was left to mere chance. There were no specific techniques available to a real estate man that would help him bring direction and order out of the vast hodgepodge of buyers and homes.

I decided to devise some time-saving methods to alleviate this situation.

First, I quit trying to sell houses to people.

## SELLING PEOPLE TO HOUSES, NOT HOUSES TO PEOPLE

With the selling-people-to-houses method the mental approach to the sales programming had to be reversed. I took the time to select very carefully one or two homes in each price category and then become a real expert about each one. I made a very thorough study

16

of the construction of the house, and its history. I learned all I could about the neighborhood. Most of all, I became totally familiar with whatever unusual features there were that caused me to select the house in the first place. Soon I had a list of special houses, and then I set out to find buyers for them, rather than following the usual procedure of finding houses for the buyers. This was a completely new approach, and I wasn't at all sure it would succeed.

### Tell one person, who will tell two, who will tell four

In my enthusiasm I found myself telling almost everyone I saw about one or more of my outstanding houses. I had something good and I knew it and I told people about it—people with whom I wouldn't ordinarily think of discussing real estate—the mailman, the service station attendant, my barber, the druggist; everyone and anyone I met. My zeal was contagious, and soon an unexpected turn of events occurred. Some of the people I had told spread the word to others. It wasn't long until I began to receive inquiries from prospects who had heard from someone who had heard from someone else about one of my special houses. The frequency of sales began to increase.

### Getting your hot listing on the community "hot line"

I was able to broaden this experiment a little further with the use of the telephone. During every call I made or received—regardless of the subject—I worked in some enthusiastic comments concerning one of the houses on my list. It wasn't long until the response convinced me that I had hit upon a winner. I had set up a person-to-person "hot line" throughout the community, and I rounded out my new technique by applying it to customers who walked into the office.

### Matching the buyer to the house is quicker than matching the house to the buyer

The success of this method was most gratifying: it made productive many hours that heretofore seemed to be wasted. The time spent house hunting was greatly reduced.

Matching the buyer to the house is much quicker than matching the house to the buyer because, when you have a pre-selected house that is the best in its category, and one buyer, it stands to reason that the time involved in bringing the two together is far less than if you have one buyer and have to hunt through ten or fifteen houses to find one that suits him.

### Third person appeal

One day some prospects were seated at my desk waiting for me to finish a telephone conversation. I was in the midst of a picturesque description of a house that I had named "the Alpine chateau." It was a stone building sitting high above the street, almost hidden by tall pine trees. It had sharply sloping roof lines, a vine-covered chimney, and recessed windows on the second floor encased by balconies. Winding steps led up to the massive double front doors, which were hung on large wrought iron hinges.

I was describing all this to my listener, and before I hung up I had made an appointment with him to see the house. Then I turned to my waiting clients. Introductions were made, and we settled into a discussion of what had brought them to the office.

It was apparent that they were preoccupied as they began to tell me the type of home they had in mind. Finally the man broke off that conversation and said,

### The indirect selling begins to work

"I'd like to hear more about the house you were describing on the telephone."

In quick succession he asked the location, price, and age of the property. With the intimate tone of the connoisseur who saves vintage wines for his close friends, I said,

"This home is one of my all-time favorites. I would be pleased to have you see it."

Hearing about this unique and charming old home had put my prospects under its spell, and I had no intention of breaking it during the drive with a discussion of such mundane matters as price, taxes and lot size. I talked of Alpine architecture, and the sound of wind in the pine trees as I remembered it from childhood. I went on to the origin and possible purpose of small balconies on second-story windows, and was deep into my theory of how the type of house has a profound effect on those who live in it, when we pulled up at our destination.

### The house sells itself

From that moment on, I said not a word. I purposely lost myself to the enchantment of this unusual home. As we waited to be invited in, I examined the large double doors, ran my fingers over the weather-worn old wood, and looked admiringly at the ancient iron doorknobs.

Once inside, I wandered slowly from room to room as one does in a museum, being sure not to lose my awestruck buyers. I examined the large brass andirons in the hearth, noted the leaded glass windows, and stopped to gaze through the huge window of the elevated living room at the panoramic view of the valley over the tops of the pine trees. There was a lovely large sunroom at the end of the house, and an equally large, bright kitchen accented with brick and burnished copper.

The enchantment was accentuated by a stained glass window visible halfway up an open semi-circular stairway. The bedrooms had the mountain lodge atmosphere so in keeping with the rest of the home, and were panelled individually in cherry wood, curly maple, pecky cypress and knotty cedar.

### A commitment that eliminated a trial closing

After an inspection of the second floor, my prospect said in a quiet voice,

"Mr. Gardiner, if the price of this home is within our means, my wife and I want to buy it."

I nodded comprehendingly, and soon we were on our way back to my office. During the drive I told them the price and they discussed the pros and cons of the purchase at some length. Their final decision was to buy the Alpine chateau.

What makes this story unusual is that when they first came into my office their intention was to purchase a bi-level, and they had expected to take two or three weeks to look at homes. It is also interesting to note that the home they bought cost exactly six thousand dollars *more* than they had intended to spend. It also generated a commission of TWO THOUSAND ONE HUNDRED SIXTY DOLLARS.

This was a thrilling experience which could only happen because I was engaged in selling people to houses.

### How this method starts a series of linked sales

Part of the never-ending excitement of the real estate business is that the next time the phone rings or the office door opens you may earn eight hundred to a thousand dollars, or more. These benefits are compounded when you have a series of sales in rapid succession. When each sale is linked to another, it is a most interesting development, because it is a series of sales that is actually created, and therefore predictable. A run-of-luck series of sales is not uncommon, but that is a different matter.

The first of my series of linked sales developed after my plan of specializing in outstanding property and my method of selling people to houses were put into practice. Because it happened, there had to be an explanation.

### Linked sales result from highly satisfied buyers who tell their friends

My explanation is that once an unusually good or an exceptionally appointed house is sold, the proud new owners become your unofficial assistants. They write letters and make innumerable phone calls, telling friends and relatives of their exciting new home. Then there is a housewarming or two, and an assortment of friends drop in to see the new home. The buyers will relate, over and over, the thrilling moments when they first saw the house, the many features that delighted them, and how they could hardly wait until the papers were signed.

The point is that *you* will be the star each time the story is told. You will become, for a little while, the greatest salesman in the world. Friends of the buyers who are also house hunting will call you, and you have an opportunity to make the second sale. If this process is repeated, as it often is, you will have a third sale. *The secret lies in having the house waiting for the buyer.*

It is most important to repeat here that the buyer must be sold to the house, and not vice versa. If you have to start on a tour of house hunting, the chain will be broken, your magical reputation will disappear, and you will be just another average real estate man.

**The music room.** I once took a listing on a lovely old colonial home with many outstanding features, but one attraction that I almost overlooked brought me not one sale, but three.

The owners had moved to another city and left the house in my care. On a visit to the property I discovered that the house had a "nothing" room. It was not a bedroom, for it had no closets; it was really too small for a den, and there was already a dining room, so I decided to call it the music room. It was off by itself on a quiet side and had a large bay window overlooking a rose garden.

### The presentation of a feature secretly
### hoped for proves irresistible

A few days later I was showing the home to a young couple. They seemed only mildly interested until I opened a door and said to the wife,

"This is the music room."

The empty house echoed with her cry of joy. She called her husband to look and, as far as she was concerned, the house was hers then and there. I had known from earlier discussion that they owned a baby grand piano and that the wife was an accomplished pianist. Two daughters were studying piano besides.

I'm sure that later she invited her many friends not to see her house, but to see her music room. It was the delight of her life and she gave me all the credit. It was just a matter of having a special house waiting for a special buyer, and it paid off to the tune of a TWELVE HUNDRED DOLLAR commission.

Shortly thereafter she sent her sister and brother-in-law to me. They bought a home and before the summer was over I had sold a home to her parents also. These were linked sales, and very little luck was involved.

### Points to remember

1. Sell people to houses, not houses to people.
2. If you have the unusual, the hard-to-find, the rare property, tell everyone you know about it—confidentially.
3. A thirty dollar feature may sell a thirty thousand dollar house.

# CHAPTER 4

# I LED THE PROSPECTS
# TO SELL THEMSELVES

---

The surest sale you'll ever make is the one where you let the prospects sell themselves. This is done by inducing the prospects to sell the house to YOU. It is a reversal of the standard method where the salesman sells the prospect, and it is not nearly as difficult as it may sound. In fact, it is an exciting technique and will cut DRASTICALLY the time necessary to make the sale.

We are striving for techniques that will (1) reduce the time involved to make a sale, allowing you to prepare for the next one, (2) make the additional, out-of-the-ordinary sale that the average real estate man overlooks or ignores, (3) carry near-misses through to completed sales.

"Reverse selling" is one of those techniques. It's nice to earn a THOUSAND DOLLARS or so while your prospects do the selling, and the time you gain will be extremely valuable in reaching the goal of a million dollars in sales.

## REVERSING THE USUAL TECHNIQUE, OR THE
## "DIRECT AND CONTROL" METHOD

This unique method of reversing roles—changing places, so to speak—whereby I became the buyer and the buyers became the real estate man, revealed many interesting insights into the minds of the buying public.

Americans are great defenders. If something or someone is unduly criticized, they take up the matter with sincere concern and defend it with increasing vigor. Applying this discovery to selling houses, and fortified with the knowledge that I was showing an exceptionally fine piece of property, I incurred very little risk in reversing the procedure by gradually and carefully becoming critical of the property. In applying the "direct and control" method, I would purposely ignore the obviously outstanding features. My buyers were puzzled by this attitude. But, because I was controlling and directing them, they were allowed to "discover" these features, and they would invariably draw them to my attention. They were taking the first step towards SELLING THE HOUSE TO ME!

### How to lead buyers to sell themselves

I channeled their thinking in the direction I had chosen by making critical comments concerning the good points of the house. They would contradict my criticism with praise. Again they were selling me. By the time the inspection was completed they defended the property almost to the point of possession. In selling me, they had sold themselves, and it was a short step to put the deal in writing.

Strange as this method sounds, it was very successful for me. It was a delight to watch it unfold, and it put zing and zest into what otherwise might have been a dull experience.

## THE CHAIN OF QUESTIONS FORMULA

The direct and control technique was used when I was working with prospects who were knowledgeable but cautious, and my object was to assure as well as to hasten their decision to buy. However, I used the chain of questions formula when I felt my prospects were fear-ridden, unsure of themselves and *not* knowledgeable in what to look for when buying a house. We arrived at the same point in approximately the same length of time, but by a different route.

### Positive answers cancel negative thoughts

I guided and directed my buyers by asking a chain of carefully conceived questions, each one of which demanded a "yes" answer.

I would start out with simple questions, and would wait for their "yes" answer. As the inspection progressed, however, and my questions grew more complex, I would not always wait for an answer. By doing this I was crediting them with knowledge. However, as we approached the end of the tour, I would revert to the more simple questions and would await their affirmative answers with deliberation. After they had said "Yes" to all the components of the property, it hardly made sense for them to say "No" when asked if they liked the house, and if they wanted to buy it.

Keeping in mind that I was offering to them one of the better houses on the market, the best way I could serve them was to allay their fears, build their confidence, and give them the necessary courage to purchase the home. In other words, I made it easy for them to buy.

## THE SILENCE TECHNIQUE

Closing is often considered a part of selling. The facts are just the reverse. Selling is a part of closing. The closing begins during the first moment of meeting with the buyers. Each small step thereafter brings closer the goal of obtaining signatures on the purchase agreement.

The closing can be broken down into these steps:

1. Getting acquainted
2. Qualifying
3. Selling
4. Signing

The silence technique is the bridge I used to move from selling to signing. Although it could probably be used to gain any rightful concession you seek at any time during the sale, it will be discussed here as a method of gaining the buyer's signature on the purchase contract. It is precise, and may require rehearsal. There are many variations of this method. I will describe the procedure I developed.

### The question that locks in your sale

When I became aware that my buyers, although willing to buy, were unwilling to sign their names to a contract, I had to depart from the standard operating procedure. I sought privacy whenever possible, because the buyers' total and undistracted attention was absolutely necessary for the silence technique to be effective.

I preferred to do my preparatory talking from a standing position while they were seated. When I was sure of their full attention, I would carefully review all the reasons why this particular property fulfilled their needs and desires. I would touch on the satisfactory possession date, the ease of financing, and the exceptionally good price.

I would pause for a second or two, and then I would say, clearly and distinctly,

"Mr. and Mrs. Buyer, let me ask you a question: is there *really* any reason why you shouldn't buy this house RIGHT NOW?"

Then I would stand motionless, not uttering a word, not moving a muscle. I let the silence do my selling.

As the silent seconds slowly ticked away, the buyers would fidget and squirm until the tension became almost unbearable. After what seems like an eternity of this, the kindest thing you can do is to hand them your pen. Remember, the first one who speaks, loses.

## EXAMPLES OF REVERSE SELLING, CHAIN OF QUESTIONS, AND "SILENT" TECHNIQUES

I stumbled upon the reverse-selling technique one day when an unusual sequence of events took place. I had run a newspaper ad over the weekend on a large, brick, tri-level home. It was a spacious home, well constructed, and surrounded by trees. It was unquestionably a good buy.

However, shortly after the ad was placed, I took a listing on what I immediately thought was one of the outstanding houses of the year. This was a long, rambling ranch house, painted a glistening white, trimmed in green. The lawn was professionally landscaped and was enclosed by a wooden fence, also painted white. The interior was a decorator's dream. I was so taken with the overall beauty of the property that I was sure the first person to see it would buy it.

### My plan to maneuver the buyer goes astray

Saturday's number one phone call was an inquiry on the brick tri-level. The callers agreed to come to the office at once and then go with me to look at the house described in the ad. I had other plans, however. I intended to show them the tri-level as rapidly as possible, then take them to the house of my choice, which I was sure they would buy on sight. It didn't work quite that way.

### The strange experience of selling a house
### I tried NOT to sell

During the showing of the house they had come to see, I by-passed the important features, and gently contradicted them when they spoke favorably concerning any aspect of the house. My impatience to get on to the ranch house provided me with my first opportunity to experience the phenomenon of reverse selling.

When the prospects told me they liked the tri-level and wanted to buy it, I was utterly amazed. I had made no effort to sell it to them. In fact, by word and action, I had actually attempted to discourage them from buying it. They had sold ME! On top of that, I earned an EIGHT HUNDRED AND TEN DOLLAR commission.

Although the situation had come about by accident, I was convinced that in the future I could recreate it by design. I had discovered another new selling technique: reverse selling.

### The chain of questions formula
### came about by experimentation

Because so many of the prospects I worked with suffered from unreasonable fears, cold feet, and procrastination, I became determined to find a way to remove these unnecessary aggravations. I tried various methods with little or no success. It came to me that the reason I was having no success was because *I* was trying to remove these problems. What I had to do was to find a way to make the buyers *themselves* eliminate them. The chain of questions formula proved to be the best solution.

### The controlling influence of the repeated "yes"

I first used this method with a couple who, during qualifying, had informed me that they had been looking at houses with other brokers for many weeks. I tried a little test question before we left the office:

"If you find the house you really like, in your price bracket, are you ready to buy it?"

They promptly answered, "Yes."

A small, but important step of commitment.

As we approached the house I hoped they would buy I asked the first of a long series of questions.

"Isn't this a nice neighborhood?"

From there on, my questions were directed to the beautiful lawn, exceptional landscaping, the neat appearance of the house, the good construction, the spaciousness of the rooms, the convenient floor plan, the ample closet space, the bright and cheery kitchen, the clean and tidy basement, the shaded back lawn, and the garage with the workshop. I spotlighted each feature with a question calculated to extract an unqualified "Yes."

To this point, everything was going well. My prospects seemed to be enjoying themselves: they were pleasant, calm, and seemingly satisfied.

If I had provided a way for them to arrest their fears, to restore their confidence in their own opinions—and if my new plan was going to be successful—I needed one more "Yes."

### Driving home the point that made the sale

I stopped the questions entirely during our ride back to the office, and visited with them in as friendly and reassuring a way as possible. I *did* control the conversation, lest they turn the tables on me with a torrent of questions which would be disastrous to my sale. Then, almost at the instant they sat down in my office, I asked them the decisive question.

"That home we just looked at certainly fills the bill for you people in every respect, doesn't it?"

The wife said, "Yes, it does."

The husband nodded affirmatively, and it was all over. No more questions, no more conversation. In less time than it takes to tell you, I had the sales contract in the typewriter. It was like writing myself a check for FIVE HUNDRED FIFTY DOLLARS, which was the commission earned.

The people who had been looking for a home for weeks and weeks had just bought one.

### The application of silence in the midst of clamor

Many versions of the silence technique have been employed in selling of all kinds over the years. When it is used to sell real estate, however, the silence technique must have special modifications. I had read a description of this procedure in a book on selling, and had seen a demonstration of it during a seminar for salesmen, but I lacked the courage to try it myself until one night when I exchanged hot and angry words with an obstinate and hard-headed buyer. It was the old story of being unable to get the buyer to sign on the dotted line.

I knew he liked the property and wanted to buy it, and he knew that I knew it. Furthermore, there was simply no reason why he should delay signing the purchase contract. As the husband and I discussed the pros and cons, the conversation became increasingly more heated. We had arrived at the loud, desk-pounding stage when the telephone rang.

I don't remember the subject of the call, but I do remember that it gave me time to think, and I realized that I would never get anywhere if I resumed the battle with my buyer. It dawned on me that I was there not to win an argument, but to sell a house.

### Recovering my composure to plan a technique

The frustration and excitement of the preceding two hours gave me the courage to make my first try at the silence technique. I made my plans quickly, and just as quickly put them into motion.

As politely and professionally as possible, I excused myself on the pretext of needing something in another part of the building. I walked into the darkened outer office, took a position against the far wall, and waited. I could see my buyers through the glass in the office door.

Five minutes went by. The husband lit his second cigarette, stood up, and began to pace back and forth. Each time he crossed in front of his wife he stopped, and they exchanged a few words. Another minute or two passed. Still I waited. I needed time to calm myself down, collect my thoughts, and rehearse precisely the timing and wording of my plan, which would make or break my sale. Finally the husband seated himself next to his wife, and they were soon involved in deep conversation. As they talked, the wife nodded her head a good deal. Then they stopped—they had talked it out.

The wife glanced at her watch, and the husband looked impatiently toward the door. I came into the office and without a word went directly to my desk. I picked up the sales contract along with the copies, rearranged them, and reread a portion. They did not say a word. Neither did I. Then I walked over and stood in front of them. I spoke a little wearily:

### The querying statement, the silence, and then the signature

"I expect you people are as anxious to get home as I am. I have just a little more to say. You love that home, it's practically made to order for you, and you can afford it. Now, I want to ask you one question: is there a single reason why you shouldn't—buy—that—house—right—now?"

Then I stood still, pen in one hand, contract in the other.

The silence was disturbed only by the wind outside, and the ticking of the wall clock. After what seemed to me an interminable period of time, the husband reached for the contract. I placed my pen in his other hand.

It was done. My first experience with the silence technique was my most unforgettable one. I was TWENTY-SEVEN THOUSAND, FIVE HUNDRED DOLLARS closer to my million dollars in sales.

### Points to remember

1. Let the buyers do the selling.
2. Keep them saying "Yes."
3. When all else fails, let the silence do your selling.
4. Remember, the first one to speak, loses.

# CHAPTER 5

# NINETY PERCENT OF MY SALES CAME FROM TEN PERCENT OF THE LISTINGS

---

As properties came on the market there were always a few that stood out far above the rest. About one house in ten, due to condition, style, price, location, or any combination of such factors, made an outstanding listing, and these I concentrated on.

I learned everything I could about the property and the neighborhood. If it had a unique history, I obtained the complete story. If it was of unusual design, such as Queen Anne Cottage, Salt Box Colonial or Tudor, I brushed up on the origin, benefits, and comforts of these various styles. If the prime factor was that it was priced below the market, I had comparable sales at my fingertips to prove it. If it was outstanding because it had had good care and was in immaculate condition, this alone was sufficient for it to be on my top 10 percent list, providing, of course, that it was priced right.

### *Know each property as if you lived there*

I visited my selected houses until I was thoroughly familiar with them, paying particular attention to the neighborhood and selecting the most pleasant route to approach the house. Revisiting the property brought to my attention excellent selling points that had escaped my observation on the first visit.

After analyzing the leading feature or features that attracted me to the house, I composed and memorized a word picture designed to create desire.

NEED and DESIRE are the TWO motivating forces in a buyer. It is reasonable to assume that the prospect brings the first of these with him. The desire must be created. This I was often able to do with vivid word pictures. When there was a house on a hill, I put a sunset behind it; when there was a fireplace, I put a fire in it; when there were bushes in the yard, I put blossoms on them. Strong desires demand fulfillment. I made sales because I had selected merchandise calculated to fulfill the need, and satisfy the desire.

### A little better than the best is unbeatable

The houses on my list generally sold quickly, often within a few days. This is not illogical because after all, in my opinion, they were the best buys on the market, PLUS having a little something extra. The secret lay, I discovered, in recognizing certain features that the buying public is seeking.

Many times the house itself was not particularly outstanding, but it had some unusual feature, as I've described in other chapters. A winding staircase, pegged floors, stained glass window, corner cupboards, outstanding landscaping, an oversize kitchen, freshly painted shutters, a stone fireplace, a panelled den, a winding walk, a rose garden, a greenhouse, a guest house, a mother-in-law apartment, a slate or tile roof, a rustic appearance, beamed ceilings—any one of these takes the house out of the run-of-the-mill category and makes it something SPECIAL in someone's eyes.

Everyone seems to want something a little better or a little different from what anyone else has, and I concentrated on those homes which, for one reason or another, were outstanding and had one or more unusual features on which a sale could be pivoted.

Often a standard listing could be elevated to my list of the top 10 percent by convincing the seller to accentuate a unique feature. My first step in selling a house was to win the confidence of the seller, and then convince him that if he *would* do his job I *could* do mine.

## THE SALE STARTS WITH THE LISTING

Listing a house properly is a job poorly handled by many real estate men. I was as guilty as any in this respect, but I was literally amazed at how easily the sale came about when I realized the importance of doing the listing job thoroughly. In the process of forcing myself to record the statistical details I came upon a remarkable discovery, one that changed the act of listing a house from a dull and boring task to a pleasant and often exciting experience.

### Houses have personalities

The discovery was that houses are not only brick and mortar, paint and lumber; they are someone's home and they reflect the personality of those who inhabit them. True, it was necessary to take down room sizes, lot sizes, taxes and other pertinent detail: this required but a few moments. Then came the pleasant experience of taking the true listing, which takes much longer. I visited the owners in the evening, when both the husband and wife have the time to enter into a relaxed conversation.

While I listened to them tell me of the portion of their lives spent in their house, they would describe the day they bought the house, what features had attracted them, and what improvements they had made. They would speak a little about their neighbors and tell me where they were going when the house was sold. As they talked about their children, their pets, and other things near and dear to them, I felt as if I were a part of the family for a little while. The house took on a personality: it became warm and friendly and I felt at home.

This was the beginning of an attitude I later carried to my buyers and has proven the theory that I have used so successfully of selling people to houses rather than houses to people.

## TOP LISTINGS CAN BE CREATED

Almost everyone in the real estate business will recognize the term "sleeper." It refers to property that is highly salable, but for some puzzling reason is overlooked by the public and the majority of real estate people. However, some individual will eventually recognize it as a sleeper and a swift sale generally takes place.

I observed this phenomenon a number of times and decided sleepers could be created. If this proved to be so, by creating them I would control them. It turned out that it was not only possible, but exciting and rewarding. Thereafter I watched for a STANDARD listing that in one way or another could be converted into a TOP listing.

### The home that offers the most or is priced the lowest will sell first

If two properties were relatively equal in all respects except that one was substantially lower priced, the one with the lower price would sell first. If two properties were priced the same, but one offered more features than the other, the one offering the most features would sell first. Therefore, if a seller needed or desired a quick sale, I could frequently convince him that the surest way to accomplish this was to adjust his price 5 to 10 percent below that of his competition. If he chose not to reduce the price, the alternative was a little more complicated, but almost equally effective. If the price was to remain unchanged, then the house must offer more or *appear to* offer more than its competition. This undertaking also had to be supported by the seller's cooperation. In the event this was denied, the property did not make my top 10 percent list and I would lay it aside.

### The best features of a house are sometimes hidden

If the cooperation was granted, I would study the property to determine what needed to be done to make it outstanding. There are as many ways to bring this about as there are houses. Sometimes one simple little change is all that is needed; sometimes a number of them; and often it takes a major revamping to get the desired effect. No attempt will be made to list all the alterations that can bring out the best points of a house, but an example or two can be given that will clarify the process.

### Five dollars worth of white paint

I once listed a brick, Cape Cod-style home where the shrubbery had been allowed to grow very high and obscure most of its beauty and charm. When the shrubbery was trimmed to normal height and the wooden shutters painted a brilliant white, this half-hidden, nondescript residence emerged to look like a small estate.

A buyer did not have to be sought. One came to me, attracted by the full view, now, of the lovely home, and five dollars worth of white paint. In this instance it was relatively easy to create a dramatic change in the appearance of a property that lifted it from near the bottom to near the top of salable merchandise.

Similar success was accomplished for other properties in other ways. Here, for contrast, is the story of the metamorphosis of a residence that needed far more drastic measures.

### Renovation that ranged from a circular drive to a rustic footbridge

During a routine group inspection of a newly listed property, I agreed with the other sales people that the listing was a "dog." It was a large, two-story residence built of fieldstone, sitting on the edge of a ravine, with the front entrance below street level and a side drive which was very difficult to enter and exit. It was in a wooded area, with most of the usable land across a ravine.

As the day wore on something about the property kept nagging at the back of my mind, and finally I decided to go back for a second look. I didn't know why, but I had a strong feeling that this property could be converted into a top listing. If I could accomplish this I would have no competition from other real estate people for a little while.

My consultation with the owner was very encouraging because he agreed that problems existed, and welcomed any suggestions that would improve the salability of his property. I had noticed that the roof was the wrong color and type. The windows were too small for such a large house, and the driveway looked dangerous and un-attractive. The grounds around the house appeared to have had no attention whatever, and the shaded, grassy area across the ravine was obviously inaccessible.

The owner set about to make the necessary corrections. At my suggestion, he had the asphalt roof covered with cedar shingles, the dropoff driveway filled in, and a horseshoe-shaped blacktop driveway built in front of the house. The brambles and underbrush among the trees surrounding the house were cleared away, and a small dilapidated wooden storage building nearby was replaced with a new one. A winding gravel path was installed from the house to the new building, separating a bird bath and bird feeder.

At the back of the house, off the living room, the owner installed a large picture window which overlooked the natural beauty of the deep ravine. Stone steps were placed from the house down to the edge of the ravine, and then a rustic footbridge was constructed to span it. Wrought iron shutters were installed on the windows, creating the illusion of greater size, and some exterior trim painting was done.

### The drab house that became someone's dream house

This all took time and money, but when it was finished and we looked at the results, the transformation was truly remarkable. I had felt that there was beauty there if we could uncover it, and we had done so.

The pleasant twist to this story is that the house was almost immediately purchased by a young couple who lived a short distance up the road. It proved to be the dream house for which they had hunted far and wide, and all the time it was hidden under their very noses. Once the charm and beauty were exposed it became a top listing and sold quickly.

## WOOING THE SELLERS

During my struggling years I had more than my share of problem sellers. They wanted too much for their house; they were uncooperative; they were pests; they were unreasonable; they were hotheads—in short, they were simply impossible. Then, one fine day, I discovered the cause of all these faults. ME. I changed me, and my attitude, and, lo and behold, most of the sellers became nice, friendly, reasonable people. Not a great deal of common sense was needed to realize the importance of being in tune with the sellers.

### Establishing a partnership with the sellers

To accomplish this, I decided to woo them. I made a special effort to visit the owners so that we might come to trust and understand one another, and to learn the role each of us was to play. Without fail, if I visited long enough, we discovered a mutual friend or hobby, or found some common ground upon which our relationship could be based. I came as a stranger, and I left as a new friend. To do this, I had to be sincere. It required that I respect their confidences, and be genuine in my intention to work diligently in their behalf.

### Continuing communication to assure cooperation

I maintained the congeniality by an occasional phone call or short visit. I informed them in advance if I intended to run a newspaper ad on their house, and followed up by mailing them a clipping of the ad. And, most important of all, after each showing of their house, I called them to discuss the comments, opinions and status of my buyers. Then, when the sale took place, if problems developed, my sellers would literally lean over backwards to do their part in working them out. Wooing the sellers helped me make additional sales more quickly and easily.

## THE THREE STEPS THAT MOVE
## A LISTING INTO THE TOP 10 PERCENT

### Step One.  Assisting the sellers in setting the price of their property

The largest problem facing real estate people today is, and probably always will be, convincing the sellers to price their house properly. The one variable that makes sense is to fit the price to the house, and not the house to the price. If it is in a secondary location it is not reasonable to move it, neither is it generally feasible to add a bedroom, dig a basement, or build a garage. So, adjust the price, not the house.

**Overpricing takes the house off the market.** The formula that I found most successful was to explain to the sellers that when they put their house on the market at a given price, their house went into competition with every other house on the market at that same price. Almost all owners want more for their house than it will bring. Yet, the same sense of values that guided them when they bought the house can be successfully appealed to if it is done patiently and properly in regards to pricing their home. Only the most obstinate will continue to resist if they are convincingly informed that they will have to take far less for their property later, if they fail to price it right in the beginning. It is a foolish owner who ignores such reasoning as,

"If you overprice your house, you're not really putting it on the market, you're taking it off."

**Price is established not by what the owner paid, but by what a buyer is willing to pay.** Another point which I frequently used, and which is calculated to cause the sellers to return to reality, is that the price they paid for a house, as well as for any improvements, does not *necessarily* dictate the price at which it will sell. I also reminded the sellers that it was not they, their friends, a real estate person, banker, or lawyer who sets the price on the house—only the buyer does that.

**If a house is overpriced the very person who would buy it will never see it.** It is an indisputable fact that any house is worth only what someone is willing to pay for it. But the most devastating effect from overpricing a house is that the very person who would buy the house will never see it. Once I could convince my sellers of the logic and truthfulness of this statement, the battle of the price was usually over.

I explained that if a house is, in fact, a $20,000 piece of property, and the sellers can prevail upon the real estate man to list it for $23,500, a buyer answering the ad on the property would be expecting the features and value of a $23,500 house; therefore, he would look and walk away. The man who is looking for a $20,000 house and saw the ad with the $23,500 price would not come to look at it; therefore, the very man who might buy the house would never see it.

If I placed a house on my selected top 10 percent list, then it had to be at a price no higher than market value; otherwise I left it for someone else to struggle with.

### Step Two.    Preparing the property
### for the market

The task of telling the sellers what must be done to spruce up their house for sale takes a certain brand of courage, but it is a task that must be undertaken or all other efforts are wasted. As always, it isn't what you say, it's how you say it that gets good results. It takes courage to tell a housewife her kitchen is not clean, and if you tell her outright you will sport a few lumps and make even fewer sales. Being a fair coward myself, I chose a way to take care of such delicate matters that seemed to get me through unscathed.

Sometime during my get-acquainted visit, as if it were routine procedure, I'd produce a sheet of paper and, after saying that I would leave a list of pointers, I'd itemize various repairs necessary to prepare the property for sale. I took care to make the first two or three items ones which would be handled by the husband. Chores such as trimming the hedge, cleaning the yard, clearing out the basement or garage headed the list.

**Talk to the wife of the seller over her husband's shoulder.** Then, as I came to the items which might reflect on the wife's housekeeping abilities, I would pause and direct my comments to the husband, although they were really meant for the wife:

"Since women do most of the house-buying, nothing seems to help a sale like an immaculate, sparkling, spic-and-span kitchen and bath."

Then, in full view of them, I would simply write on the list, 'Kitchen', 'Bath'. I would continue my list with painting to be done, screen doors to be fixed, and so forth. And again I would attempt to be subtle. I would say, this time to the wife,

"I will try to call you far enough in advance of a showing so that you will have time to make the beds, pick up the children's toys and, in general, put the house in order."

I'd end this part of the conversation by telling them that I had learned that a house which was fresh and clean, neat and orderly, invariably sold more quickly and brought the asking price more often than did a house where no effort was made to prepare it for sale.

### Step Three.  The sellers' role
### during the showing of the house

After I had lost a few sales because the sellers said or did the wrong thing, I decided to make my sellers aware of how critical the role was that they were to play, and how important it was that they play it as I instructed them.

I opened this topic by explaining that since they would be paying me for selling their house, they should let me do the selling. I explained that my buyers had confidence in me and would believe what I told them; but that they would feel that statements by the sellers were prejudiced and therefore not necessarily true. I asked my sellers to volunteer no information whatsoever: in fact, even if they heard me inadvertently answer a buyer's question erroneously, they were absolutely not to correct me in the presence of the buyers, but to call me later. I informed them that the ideal way that they could assist in a sale was to disappear after greeting us at the door. I further asked that all pets and children be under control, all radios and television sets be off, blinds and drapes be open in the daytime, and all lights in all rooms be on at night.

**Precise instructions for the sellers if the buyers return on their own.** I also warned them that, in the event my buyers returned on their own, under no circumstances were they to discuss price or volunteer information, however helpful they might consider it to be. They should be courteous, of course, and invite them to take another look around; however, the property and the price must be discussed only with me. Otherwise, something like this could happen:

We were standing on the rear lawn discussing the house we had just inspected. My buyer paused for a moment and said, "Mr. Gardiner, I like this house, I want to buy it."

In keeping with the best selling technique, I led her back into the house, headed for the front door so as to get her in my car as quickly as possible, and take her to the office to draft the contract. We didn't quite make it.

**The seller's well-intended remark lost the sale.** The lady of the house, who had evidently overheard the buyer's statement, stopped us in the living room and uttered the fatal words,

"Mrs. White, one of the things you will like about this neighborhood is that none of the little children ever come over to play unless their mothers call me first."

Words well meant, but they killed the sale. We were no sooner seated in my car than the lady said,

"Forget it, Mr. Gardiner. I have no intention of living in a neighborhood where I'm expected to be a social secretary for my six-year-old daughter."

Ridiculous? Certainly, but it happened. It's only one of dozens of ridiculous cases where a comment volunteered by a seller lost a sale. The sellers, by their position, are on the defensive, and they cannot win in a discussion of their own property with the buyer. Sooner or later they will say the wrong thing, and often it's sooner. I eliminated this problem almost completely by rehearsing my sellers in the role they were to play, and insisting that they stick to the script.

### Points to remember

1. Of the houses for sale, work on the best, and pass up the rest.
2. The battle of the price should be fought when the house is listed.
3. Look for ways to raise the value and not the price.
4. Woo the seller and win the sale.
5. Train your seller to be a SILENT partner.

# CHAPTER 6

# THE SHORT SPEECH THAT URGES PROSPECTS TO MAKE A DECISION AND THE COUNTER ACTION TO USE IF THEY DON'T

When you have prospects who are ready, willing, and able to buy, and you have shown them property that you know they want to buy but you can't get them to admit it, you have a problem. Forcing prospects to *make* a decision is difficult, but getting them to ADMIT they have made a decision is sometimes even more so. By refusing to admit they have reached a decision to buy, what the prospects have done is given you an *unspoken* "We want to think it over." It is a frustrating and formidable situation. I resolved it with the use of a short, stinging, irrefutable speech. Bear in mind that the people really WANT the home, but they think there is some benefit in waiting a while before they buy it. To keep them from running the risk of losing it, it is YOUR responsibility to move them to make a decision to buy it *now*. That's the purpose of the short speech.

## THE SHORT SPEECH

"Mr. and Mrs. Smith, I have something of the utmost importance to discuss with you. We have agreed that this home suits you in every way. Now we have reached that psychological moment when

41

you must make a decision. For some reason, you are delaying making that decision. All of our time, all of our effort, and all of our searching has been leading to this moment. If we let it pass without your decision it could cause you great harm. You know and I know there is not one feasible reason why you shouldn't buy this home right now.

### Why they should decide one way or the other RIGHT NOW!

"A decision, of course, may be positive or negative. In just a minute I'm going to ask you to MAKE that decision, and here is the reason why. If you don't decide to buy this home now, chances are you will *never* buy it. It just seems to work that way. You have been good enough to put your trust and confidence in me up till now, and I hope you believe that I would not destroy my good reputation as a real estate man by giving you poor advice in order to make this one sale.

"Time after time I've seen people allow this psychological moment of decision to pass, never to have it return. There are many reasons why this happens, but they're really immaterial here. The important point for you to know is that you should not leave undecided a matter so vital to you and your family. You owe it to me, but, even more, you owe it to yourself to heed my advice when I tell you that the probability of your *ever* owning this home depends on the decision you're going to make *right now*." (Momentary pause) "Many things can happen by tomorrow and I know you people don't want to lose this house, now, do you? What's your decision, shall I draw up the contract?"

That's the essence of the short speech. I have found it very effective because it is the TRUTH! Procrastinating buyers DO lose out.

### There is a technique designed for every problem

If, however, they *still* insist they want to think it over, at least they've made their decision and not left you in a quandary. In that event, you simply use the technique described in Chapter 13, "Creating a Crisis." Nevertheless, remember there is only one time you will ever make a sale and that's NOW! Not tomorrow or the day after, but NOW! Trust welcomes advice, so advise them well.

### Some of the perplexities concerning home buyers

Prospects and the myriad problems they present must be studied closely so that the proper remedy from your bag of techniques may be administered. The games buyers play are often a mystery. Why, for instance, will they decide to buy a certain home but refuse to say so? Why will they silently stall a $25,000 purchase over a $50 objection? Can anyone tell me why people will decide to look for a home, then, when they find it, hesitate to buy it?

These were the perplexing questions I wrestled with that eventually brought about the short speech, uncovered the hidden qualification, and pointed to the need for the 'shakedown'.

If you earn that $800 to $1,000 commission tonight, you can spend tomorrow working toward the next one. That's part of the secret of selling a million dollars worth of real estate in one year.

## THE HIDDEN QUALIFICATION

The old standards, "ready, willing, and able," must be supported by a fourth qualification. Prospects MUST be communicative. I had to develop a certain trust and confidence to reach this plateau of intimate communication. At first I believed that if a buyer were willing to buy, he would say so. This entire matter needed deep study, but a specific incident brought home to me the importance of communication from the prospects to the salesman in order to consummate a sale.

### On being stymied by noncommittal buyers

I had shown a young family a few homes, all of which met their needs and desires, and they seemed very interested in one of them. We discussed the property thoroughly, and at the proper time I asked them if they wanted to buy the house.

They answered neither yes nor no. I was certain they were ready, willing and able to buy, but they absolutely would not commit themselves. In fact, most of their contribution to the conversation was silence. They sat as if waiting for something to happen. After a couple of hours of getting nowhere, they left for their home, disappointed, I am sure. I departed for mine, perplexed and bewildered. My state of confusion continued after I arrived home, until suddenly I had an inspiration which prompted me to telephone my buyers then and there.

### The power of a professional opinion

My first words were, "Mr. Brown, *I* think you should buy that house on Seventh Street."

His agreement was almost immediate, and in thirty minutes we were back at the office and the purchase agreement was signed. Then my curiosity got the better of me and I asked the Browns why they hadn't bought the house earlier in the evening. They said that they were waiting for me to *tell* them they *should* buy it. I had asked them only if they *wanted* to buy it. They considered me a professional, respected my opinion and wanted me to tell them that to buy the house was the right thing for them to do.

There it was—an undeniable lack of communication—intimate communication which goes beyond the broad meaning of the word as used in general business relationships, and places it on a very personal plane. As they sat in my office earlier in the evening, the Browns had been silent because they were waiting for me to tell them that they would be doing the right thing to buy the house. They wanted me to share in the responsibility of making their decision. I had failed them. It was the last time I ever failed this particular responsibility.

### The difference between a willing buyer and a committed one

I came to understand that many people were *willing* to do this or that, but did not actually *do* it. Now I understood that having willing buyers did not *guarantee* that they would buy. They often needed reassurance. Sometimes they wanted to discuss a very personal problem, a problem that was their only stumbling block, but they would not broach the subject. I had to seek them on this intimate level of communication and extend my professional reassurance. Even though they were willing, many times formidable obstacles of a personal nature had to be dealt with before their willingness could be converted into action. *And action is the big word.*

When I added 'communication' to the qualifying steps, I was able to take my buyers beyond the point of being *willing* to the point of being *committed*. The hidden qualification was a secret key.

## NEEDS VERSUS ABILITY TO PAY

To sell a piece of real property, I learned, many factors must be brought into a delicate balance. Whenever I had a stubborn situation where all indications toward a quick and easy sale were not productive, a search for the element which was out of balance frequently revealed that the prospects' desires were greater than their ability to pay; or the reverse, that their ability to pay was higher than the price bracket in which they were looking. In these situations, some notable adjustments are required if a sale is to be made.

### Produce an acceptable compromise

Where inability to pay was the problem, a compromise was mandatory. Usually a serious discussion with my prospects settled the matter. I would show them that the best way to handle their predicament was to purchase a home priced within their means and use it as a stepping stone to the home they most desired or needed. Accumulated savings, a growing equity, and increase in income would make it possible for them to step up into a better home every two or three years until they reached the quality level that they were seeking.

### How to squelch well-to-do bargain hunters

The reverse situation presented a more formidable obstacle. Buyers who could afford a far better home than those in the price range in which they were looking could waste a lot of my time. It was a great temptation to stick with prospects of good financial standing, but it was apparent that unless I could get their needs and desires in balance quickly, I was far better off to pass them by. I would explain to them that their wish to make a low expenditure was pulling in the opposite direction from their natural desire for a better home that would give them satisfaction, comfort, and pride, in keeping with their financial position.

It was an impasse: as long as this condition existed, the odds against their buying *any* home were great. Until I was able to put their mental faculties to work digesting and analyzing this reasoning, I was wasting my time. In most cases, after thinking it over seriously, they would agree with me, forget their bargain-hunting, and a sale would be made without further delay. The factors were back in balance.

### Temper their desires but fulfill their needs

When buyers went over their heads, so to speak, in their insistence on luxury they could not afford, I could usually appeal to their common sense by explaining that practical features would have to take precedence over intrinsic desires. I started one family on the road to owning the precise home they wanted by way of the stepping-stone method.

**How dream houses are constructed.** At our first meeting, the wife eagerly detailed her version of their proposed home. She described a one-story house with a large kitchen, two baths, four bedrooms, a fenced lot, shade trees, a good neighborhood, and close to schools and shopping.

Her husband then explained what he wanted most: a basement, a garage, a blacktop driveway, a fireplace, and a room for a workshop. I had listings that would fulfill all of these requirements.

**Convincing them to take a wayside cottage on the road to the dream home.** During the qualifying time, however, it became apparent that they were far short of having the necessary down payment, nor did they have an income large enough to meet the mortgage payments. These conditions called for a drastic compromise, but their good sense and faith in themselves as well as a willingness to accept my explanation made a compromise house possible, albeit it was a far cry from what they wanted. They accepted it because they understood that it was the first of three or possibly four houses that they would own on their way to their heart's desire. And it was the *only* way they could obtain it.

**Choose well, for the resale is your responsibility.** The resale factor as well as the price had to be the prime considerations. The home we finally settled on was a brick two-story with a tiny kitchen, one bath, no basement, no garage, no workshop, and a gravel drive. But it was well constructed, priced right, it served their basic needs, and they could afford it.

About every two and a half to three years thereafter I had an almost automatic sale, in fact two sales, as I would sell the house they lived in, and help them find one a little better. I filled their need by tempering their desires.

## IF THEY DON'T NEED WHAT THEY WANT, MAKE THEM WANT WHAT THEY NEED

There are other "problem buyers" whose situation may resemble somewhat the one we have just covered, but in reality the two are far removed. These buyers have problems, but don't know it and won't believe it if they are told. They might be called dreamers. They build houses in their minds with a hodgepodge of inconsistency. They are the ones who start out by saying they want five acres of land, and wind up their requirements fifteen minutes later by saying they want to be adjacent to the downtown area. I have actually been told by buyers that they wanted a one-floor house, and later that the second floor *must* have a bath. They will request features inside the house that would make construction impossible.

### Castles in the air can't be lived in

Over a period of time they will admire one feature in one friend's house, another in another, and so on. Then, when they set out to buy, they are determined to incorporate all of these things in their new home.

They give no thought to the monstrosity which the accumulation of all these features would create. They will insist they want such items as three-sided fireplaces, island kitchens, darkrooms, a room to paint in, a room to read in, a room to sew in, aquarium room dividers, circular entrances or foyers, colonnaded entrances, greenhouses, lily ponds, Roman baths, weathervanes, and on and on. Many of these features individually are fine: even a number of them together would be in good taste; however, it's obvious that *some* restraint must be exercised.

Most of the unusual items which they say they want are the ones they do not need. I simply took the time to discuss each unreasonable item until they admitted they really didn't need it. And, I suspect, if the truth were known, they really didn't want it. One by one, we eliminated each one until finally I was able to convince them to *want what they needed*. Again, the factors were in balance, and a sale was in the making.

### The convertible versus the family sedan theory

Another time-waster is the family that sets out to buy a home, but decides to sightsee for a little while first. With the full knowledge that they are going to buy a home that will give them the most for their money, devoid of extras, trimmings and unneeded features, they will first look at homes either above their price class or filled with so much gingerbread that they know they would never buy them. They enjoy the thrill and excitement of visiting home after home filled with new gadgets, expensive carpeting and drapes, and luxurious appointments. After a few days or weeks of this they will settle down and buy the kind of house they knew they would in the beginning.

They have fooled a lot of people in the meantime: I tried not to let them fool me. I simply let them indulge their fancy on their own. I kept in touch with them, and when I sensed they were ready to get down to serious business, I was ready.

I've always compared this type of buyer to the man who goes forth to buy a car, and looks with great longing at the sporty convertible, but always returns with the old, dependable family sedan.

## THE SHAKEDOWN PERIOD

As I strove for those additional sales that would lead to a big year, it became apparent that I, too, had decisions to make. Since the so-called "normal" sales rolled along smoothly and steadily, I had to glean the extra sales from the unusual and out-of-the-ordinary situations or buyers and do it in a short period of time. Somewhere, after becoming involved with unusual buyers, or buyers with unusual demands, I had to requalify them. I called this the *"shakedown."* I had to put the factor that was out of balance, back in balance immediately and precisely. Until I did, I was wasting time I could not afford to spare.

### It is imperative to be able to tell a prospect from a "suspect"

To review, the problem might be that the prospects were looking at homes above their price range, or they were seeking a property with incompatible or impossible features. Maybe they were bargain hunters. Sometimes they were poorly advised. Possibly they had personal problems that they were reluctant to discuss. Often they lacked communication between themselves. Frequently they were indulging in a house-looking spree. Perhaps they needed someone to share in the responsibility of making their decision. Prospects such as these are legitimate buyers if the problems can be overcome.

The perennial prospects, the Sunday afternoon lookers, those with no down payment, those looking for a house for a friend or relative, and those who have a house to sell first are not buyers and I eliminated them during the *first* qualification period.

*If you permit the right moment to pass, forget it: it's too late.*

When the psychological moment comes for the shakedown or re-evaluation, chances for success diminish rapidly if the moment is allowed to pass. Take whatever action is indicated: take it strong and take it immediately, or your sale will die before your eyes.

### Points to remember

1. Prepare a potent short speech.
2. Establish intimate communication with the buyers.
3. Be willing to share the responsibility of their decision.
4. Guide and direct your buyers every step of the way.
5. Eliminate the wall of incompatibility.
6. Have the courage to shake down problems.

# CHAPTER 7

# SOMETIMES IT PAYS TO GET MAD

---

You can't afford to lose a single sale if you intend to sell $1,000,000 of real estate in one year. If your average sale is $25,000 and if you lose four of those in 12 months, you've lost $100,000, a tenth of a million. Lose one a month and you've lost a third of your million. I'm not talking about sales you didn't make. I'm talking about sales you had (although you may not have realized it), and then lost.

### If true buyers won't sign a sales agreement, you didn't miss a sale, you lost it

Struggling to make or create a sale is one thing, but when you and your client have successfully taken all the steps usually considered adequate to bring about a sale, then in THEORY you HAVE your sale, but in FACT you don't, due to the unreasonable reactions of your buyers when the time comes for them to express their intent. In other words, they should have bought but didn't. Therefore, if some step isn't taken to handle the buyers, the sale you theoretically have will never come about. Thus, in my way of looking at it, it is a lost sale.

There are ways to recapture lost sales. One way is good, old-fashioned anger. Get hopping mad! You had a sale, and it has been taken away from you. If the circumstances indicate it, blow your top! But in a way calculated to *make* the sale.

You've done your job and you've done it well. You're entitled to be paid. If you have an unreasonable, illogical, uncooperative buyer, you can often salvage your sale if you get good and mad. But this anger must not be misapplied. It must be controlled. We're going to talk a little about that.

## IF THEY WON'T LISTEN TO REASON, GIVE THEM REASON TO LISTEN

From time to time I would find myself involved with a lost sale: that is, a sale that was made, but for which I would never collect a commission, because my buyers would not cooperate by permitting the normal closing procedure to take place. This I could not tolerate. Drastic problems required drastic steps. In this case I found nothing worked so well as getting mad. Actually, literally, letting my temper fly. The shock value upon my buyers was remarkable. They were caught by surprise and the impact of my righteous anger would do the trick. The types of buyers we are discussing fall into four categories:

1. The dawdlers
2. The infatuated ones
3. The professional complainers
4. The unpredictables

### The dawdlers

Sometimes for hours, even for days, dawdlers concern themselves with features unimportant and even unrelated to the property they are going to purchase. They are such great talkers that even the strongest real estate man finds it impossible to keep the line of thought directed toward the ultimate signing of a purchase contract. They will buy, but only when they have run down and are worn out. They sometimes go on for days. You can't afford this expense of *time*.

### The infatuated ones

These prospects simply love to look at houses; it is almost a sport with them. With apparently genuine interest they will inspect and discuss at great length every house shown to them. Regardless of price, size, or style they will exhibit a great liking for homes that under no circumstances would they actually purchase. It would take someone with a crystal ball to learn which house they would ultimately buy. *They* know but have no intention of indicating which one it is as long as they are indulging their infatuation to "just look at homes."

They are using the time you need to earn an income for recreational purposes. STOP THEM!

### The professional complainers

Probably the most easily recognized are the professional complainers. They raise objections to a house before they have even seen it. They get around to expressing their opinion rather quickly that the cost of everything in general is too high: utilities are too high, taxes are too high, repairs are too high, and most certainly the cost of houses is too high. They claim builders cut corners, servicemen cheat, no one can be trusted. They are pessimists filled with suspicion and distrust. They tear apart everything you show them. *They need your help*.

### The unpredictables

Buyers of this type either like everything shown to them or nothing at all. They seem to change horses in the middle of the stream, and do it often. They will approve a feature in one house and disapprove of the same feature in another. Their comments and actions will lead you to believe that they are absolutely sold on a certain house, but they always want to look at a few more. They believe the next home they see will be a little better—this could go on forever. They want you to sell them a home and at the same time are scared to death that you will.

All of these people are buyers, but they won't buy because they are out of control. You have taken them through the normal steps to a sale, but because of their individual peculiarities they will not only resist and avoid your closing, but are often oblivious of it. You will run up against this quite often in a year's time. Each one represents a sale, *which need not be lost*.

### I USED CONTROLLED ANGER

The buyer who is off course can be returned to a state of normal thinking by the use of controlled anger, so, GET MAD. Slam home your points loud and clear. Get their attention. Make them listen to reason. You have nothing more to lose—the sale is already lost—this is one way to regain it. Your anger should be genuine, *but it must be controlled.*

By using this method you are doing your job better and you are proving yourself a professional because these types of prospects need assistance above and beyond that given to others. If you fail them, their search for a home will be unreasonably long, their perspective will be warped and they probably will make a bad buy.

The anger technique, to produce the best results, should be applied step by step in the following sequence.

**1. Preparation.** Review the events up to the moment. You must be sure you're right. If you have not overlooked anything, if you have done your job but the buyers have not done theirs, then you have earned a commission, *but you will never collect it unless you take charge of the situation.* You are going to use a very unorthodox selling technique—you're going to be forceful—you're going to get mad. You have to be mentally prepared for this step, because your anger must be genuine and it must be controlled, *because once you start there's no turning back.*

**2. The setup.** Once again start to close, only this time, somewhere along the line at a point of your choosing, get their complete attention. If you're in the car, you might suddenly pull to the curb and stop; or you can do it by changing the tone of your voice. Suddenly, in a loud, firm and commanding tone of voice, say,

"MR. AND MRS. JONES, I THINK IT'S ABOUT TIME WE HAD A TALK!" If necessary, repeat it. Once you have their attention, then it's time to get angry.

**3. Express anger in your own way.** How you handle the situation depends upon which of the four problem buyers you're dealing with. Remember, you have a right to be mad. You have done a job and you're not going to be paid for it. To be angry is perfectly natural.

We all express our anger in different ways. In my case it would follow a pattern something like this:

"We just don't seem to be getting anywhere. I want to help you make the best buy I can but you won't let me. You won't listen to me—you don't pay attention. You talk as if you knew more about the real estate business than I do.

"We could go on like this for days, and I can't afford that. If you want to buy a house with my assistance, THEN DO SO! If you want to play games and run the show and waste time, then you're on your own. I have other important business to take care of, and unless you listen to my advice I simply can't help you. It's up to you what you want to do, but we're going to decide right here, and right now! I appreciate your business, I don't mean to be rude, but I cannot be of service to you unless we become more compatible and harmonious.

### There's only one thing left to do and that's buy it

"Look at what's happened up till now. I have shown you some good homes—one that is right for you in every respect. You know it and I know it. We've examined it from every angle. We've discussed all the pros and cons. You know, in every way, it's the right home for you. There's simply no logical reason to prolong this matter any further. There's only one thing left to do, and that's buy it! Nobody knows that better than you do. So I suggest we quit fooling around like irresponsible children and buy this home!"

In the ensuing silence, take the necessary steps to draft a sales agreement. They will either sign it or they won't: I'm wagering they *will*.

### When you've reached your goal—ease off

Of course the intensity and direction of the angry speech varies with the circumstances. By watching the reaction of the buyer it can be stopped at any time. Do so if it becomes apparent that the goal of bringing them under control has been reached. After all, the primary purpose is not to indulge your temper but to make the sale!

This is not a technique for the timid salesman. But if you're convinced this drastic step is justified, then:

A. Challenge your buyer's judgment and common sense as measured by the practical and reasonable methods of purchasing a home used by the buying public in general.

B. Inform them of the fact that your job is done. You have fulfilled their needs and desires.

C. Make it crystal clear that you are a professional businessman whose stock in trade is his time and knowledge, and you have given adequately of both.

D. Demand that when you have submitted a property well qualified to suit their needs, they weigh the pros and cons of that property with a rational mind and give you a well-contemplated "yes or no" answer.

### Sprinkle your anger with friendliness

You will have to use your own judgment on how long to talk and how severe to get. Once you've made your point that you don't intend to put up with any more foolishness, then conclude your remarks by tempering the anger with a sprinkling of friendliness. Let your voice return to normal. Maintain a tone of finality with the threat of abandonment if they resist your advice.

Remember, this is an all-out, make-or-break technique. You'll either have a sale or you won't, but in either event you will know which it is quickly.

My first use of anger with a prospect was *not* planned or controlled, *but it was successful,* and when I reviewed how my strategy had worked in completing another sale, as I always did, I added controlled anger to my handbook of selling methods.

### The know-it-all-doctor

From the very first minute the good doctor and his wife came into the office I knew I was in for a rough time. He completely dominated the conversation, resisted the get-acquainted preliminaries, and would not let his wife answer any questions. He described precisely the kind of house he wanted, but ignored my questions about price range or location. In effect, he dared me to find a house that would please him. My dislike for him rose like a Death Valley thermometer. I decided to accept the challenge.

**A buyer often says "no" because he doesn't know.** I knew of a home I believed this man would buy if I handled it right. It met his stipulations about quality and size, and a panelled room behind the attached garage offered him an excellent private office. But almost before we stopped in the driveway, his criticism started. He objected to the style, the location, the grounds—but I noticed he inspected the panelled room more than once.

To his surprise, this was the only house I showed him. It was the best I had and there would have been no purpose in showing him the second best. But the doctor's flow of criticism and objections was unceasing during the drive back to my office. Like the lady in *Hamlet,* he protested too much, and I suddenly realized that he *did* like the house and actually wanted to buy it. To test my conviction I drove him back to see the house once again, and this time was met with silence but finally a grudging inquiry about the price.

"More than it is worth," he said.

The doctor called me often during the next few days, but each time he insisted that he was not interested in buying the house. I was drained of patience—and of ideas how to bring this man to the point of decision.

**The inevitable showdown.** A chance meeting on the street brought about an unrehearsed and unexpected showdown. The sight of the doctor reminded me of all the time I had spent so uselessly trying to help him. My temper flared, and the outburst began.

It covered his unreasonable attitude toward purchasing a house that obviously fulfilled his needs, had the exact features he wanted, was priced right, *and that he clearly liked.* He was reminded that he had come to me and asked me to do a job, which I had done and done well. He was assured that no more of my time would be wasted with him. Then I concluded my tirade by driving home a most important point: I predicted that he would search the town and not find another home that suited him nearly as well and that ultimately, through sheer exhaustion and befuddled perspective, he would buy something far less satisfactory. My final words were,

"Doctor, why don't you stop this monkey business and buy this house NOW?"

Anger turned the trick. In an hour he was in my office, and from then on it was one of the easiest sales I ever had.

I'll never forget the day I operated on the doctor and earned $2,250.

### The whimsical newlyweds

This young couple liked EVERYTHING about EVERY house I showed them. They finally seemed to settle on one home and I thought I had the sale in the bag, but when we approached the dotted line business they hauled out that old sales killer,

"We'd like to think it over."

They were most convincing, and I fell for it. My ears were filled with assurances that they KNEW this was the house for them. It was so nice, so attractive, they just loved it, they were going to be so happy there, they were going to buy it, but—they wanted to think it over. They would be back the first thing in the morning, and would I have the papers all ready for them to sign? They left. I went home, confident that I had the commission in my pocket.

**From enchantment to rejection overnight.** Bright and early the next morning they returned, eager and excited. But something was wrong; there was no mention of their dream house of the day before; no talk of their plans to furnish it; no readiness to sign the papers.

They wanted to look at more houses! I was bewildered. I asked about the house they had fallen in love with the day before. The husband nonchalantly replied that they had decided overnight they really didn't like it after all. I took them out once more to find a house that would please them.

That day and one or two following were carbon copies of the first, and I let them snow me with their youthful exuberance. When I left them each afternoon they had found a dream house; when I saw them the next morning the burning desire was ashes, and they were all set to look some more.

**The switch from considered indulgence to controlled anger.** Finally I had had my fill. When I saw them walk into the office still another morning, I was, instantly, fighting mad. I ushered them into a private office, motioned them to sit down, glared at them for a silent moment and asked:

"Will you kindly tell me what in thunder is going on?"

For the next few minutes I reviewed their behavior up to then. I described their childishness, their evident desire to play games with me, their inability to make a decision. I reminded them that they were entering a grown-up world when they took on the responsibilities of being homeowners, and it would require more stability than they had shown up to this point.

**Following up the verbal punch with a friendly pat on the head.** Toward the end of my speech I tempered my tone a good deal, as I had with the doctor. I said that as a professional real estate man I could help them make their decision and would be happy to do so. I felt the best home for them was the first one we had looked at, and offered to take them back for a second look, but I stated firmly that I had no more time to spare playing games. Then I left them alone to discuss the matter between themselves.

Their decision was to buy the house, and to the best of my knowledge they're living there today. Straight talk and controlled anger settled them down. They owned a nice home and a TWELVE HUNDRED DOLLAR commission was earned. Although it had been some months since I had flared up at the doctor, I knew that controlled anger was a selling technique I could use if it was applied appropriately.

### The overwhelming executive

If a prospect leads the salesman around by the nose, there is very little chance of making a sale. The first time this happened to me, it was accomplished by an expert.

He was impressive and I was taken in by his captivating personality. He completely controlled me before I realized it. *It should have been the other way around.* He was a self-styled expert on everything—real estate, home construction, what was wrong with the city, the state, the national government. The house he was looking for would have to be outstanding, he said, and price was no object. He described what he wanted so positively and in such detail that I felt he would find the house and I was just along to do the driving.

**A buyer completely out of control.** When I took him to two or three exceptional properties, he didn't stop talking long enough to really take a look at them. Without breaking his stream of words he dismissed each house with a flick of his hand. After a few days of this I finally came to my senses and it made me MAD. Not at the prospect, but at myself for letting myself be taken in. When he came in the next morning I had taken the ring from my nose, and I was ready for him. I quickly settled the question of 'price is no object' by telling him of an estate that had everything he was looking for, priced at $165,000. He protested that that was far too much. Then he was on the defensive and I kept him there.

**Bring him firmly back in line.** He'd been running the show for too long, I said, and now my turn had come. I knew nothing about the value of homes or the type of construction in his home town, and didn't give a hoot, but I did know the features, styles and values of the homes in our area. I made it clear that I was in a far better position to advise him than he was to advise me. I put it in plain words that I did not intend to leave the office until we agreed on who was the expert. I was going to sell and he was going to buy and both events were going to take place quickly! I promised him that I would do everything I could to help him find a suitable home at a fair price, but it had to be done my way or not at all. Otherwise we were both wasting our time.

He smiled, agreed, and said, "Let's go."

We had no further trouble. Late that night he signed a purchase contract for a $45,000 home and gave me a check for more than twice the amount of deposit required.

**The golden worth of referrals.** An interesting development from this sale was that in the months and years to come this man sent me many people who were transferred to the area by his company and, without a single exception, they each bought a home above $30,000. All in all I believe he was responsible eventually for $10,000 in commissions. And all because I got mad.

But a word of caution—although the controlled anger technique added six or eight sales to my million dollar year that I would not have had otherwise, I want to repeat that I only used it if I felt it served the best interests of my clients, and then discreetly. I never want to forget that people pay me a very high compliment when they become my customers, and it is my obligation to serve them well.

## SUMMARY OF THE EVENTS RELATED IN EXAMPLES

1. In the Case of the Know-It-All-Doctor, this was the moment of discovery of the usefulness of the "controlled anger" technique.

    a. The doctor fell into the category of the professional complainer.

    b. By every standard of selling procedure the deal with the doctor should have been made quickly and easily, but I just couldn't consummate it.

    c. My frustration, puzzlement and disappointment culminated in anger, which was the very thing that caused the whole sale to jell.

    d. I had discovered a powerful selling agent but, like an explosive, it had to be properly handled.

2. The Case of the Whimsical Newlyweds.

    a. They were the first of the "infatuated ones" that I submitted to the controlled anger technique.

    b. This type is so akin to the professional complainers in their time-wasting distrust of themselves that they responded in an almost identical manner.

    c. After hours and hours of trying to "sell" them a home, a few minutes of anger laid to them with discretion brought a sale.

    d. A $1,200 commission was the result of this unorthodox method.

3. The Overwhelming Executive was of the "unpredictable" breed.

    a. By now I had acquired a little experience with this volatile technique.

    b. He responded to my calculated anger so readily it convinced me of the value of this extraordinary strategy.

    c. It can be used whenever a prospect unreasonably withholds a decision to buy when under normal circumstances a normal or standard prospect would do so.

    d. I have brought many a "dawdler" to bay with the method and added THOUSANDS OF DOLLARS to my income. With the Executive alone it earned TWO THOUSAND SEVEN HUNDRED DOLLARS commission.

### Points to remember

1. It's okay to lose your temper in order not to lose the sale.
2. Remember to keep some method in your madness; i.e., use *controlled* anger.

3. The unexpected force of anger will bring the disorganized thinking of your various prospects into sharp focus.

4. If you're willing to give them hell, be willing also to give them help.

# CHAPTER 8

# HOW I CORRECTED MY
# BIGGEST MISTAKE

---

"Bob made $24,000 last year." I overheard the statement and it kept running through my mind like the words of a song. For the same period my earnings were a little over $8,000. I couldn't understand the big difference. The more I thought about it the more it bugged me.

Bob occupied the desk next to mine. As I looked over at him my thought was, what does he have that I don't? What's his big secret? If I could find out I could obviously triple my income. Taking a sheet of paper, I started a list.

| | |
|---|---|
| OFFICE | Same |
| NUMBER OF HOURS ON THE JOB | Same |
| NUMBER OF LISTINGS TO WORK WITH | Same |
| EDUCATION, APPEARANCE, AGE | Approximately the same |
| AMOUNT OF EFFORT EXTENDED | Same |
| EARNINGS | NOT the same |

It should have added up, but it didn't. What was the element that made the difference? The more I studied the list the more I was sure the fault lay with me. Somewhere I was making a mistake. When I discovered what it was I went on to sell one million dollars worth of real estate in one year.

## THE BIG LITTLE DIFFERENCE

What I sought was not an obvious thing that could be pinpointed and corrected, such as a faulty technique or the improper handling of prospects. It was invisible, intangible, and aggravatingly elusive.

### The discovery of PSA

The answer didn't come like a flash of light; instead, it emerged slowly like sunlight from behind a hill. It started one day when I overheard Bob on the telephone. He was talking to the owners of a home we had listed, telling them that he planned to show their home that afternoon and that he should have the sales contract prepared and ready for their signature by early evening. I was astounded! He hadn't even shown the house yet! *But in his mind it was sold!* There simply was no doubt about it. He was matter-of-fact, but absolutely confident that his prospects would sign a purchase contract on the home. He was so sure of himself, his product, and his buyer that in his mind the sale was already made. He KNEW he had a sale. If I had been handling the prospects I would have HOPED I had a sale. THERE was the little difference that made the big difference. But how did he know that he had a sale? Because he had a Positive Selling Attitude!

### From an ordinary to a master salesman

With all my hard work, with all my determination, and with all my varied techniques, without an understanding and ultimate adoption of this Positive Selling Attitude there is no doubt that I would still be earning $8,000 to $10,000 a year.

Whether Bob made that particular sale or not is of no consequence. The point is that at the end of a year, all other things being the same, he produced three times the number of sales that I did. Once I recognized this attitude of total confidence, I had to come to understand it better so that I might acquire it.

In one way it seemed to me a matter of allowing a sale to happen, rather than having me chasing after it. When I compared my mental attitude with Bob's, the difference was so apparent I wondered why I hadn't discovered it sooner. It was what separated a master salesman from an ordinary one.

Let us look at the effect upon the prospect of the two different selling personalities. The positive against the negative, so to speak.

## NSA

The person with a negative selling attitude will push his selling points just a tiny bit too hard. The strain of eagerness to make a sale will run along the edge of his conversation. Fervently hoping they will buy will betray him into answering a question just a little too hastily. By his actions and in his tone of voice, so slight as to be almost, but not quite, unnoticeable, he will create a feeling in the minds of his prospects that *his making the sale has become more important than their buying the house.* In other words, if the prospects believe the real estate man is trying to make a sale, their acceptance of the truthfulness of his words will begin to wane. Then, when the buyers arrive at the point of making a decision, this negative selling attitude seeps out of the hopeful salesman, and causes the buyers to hesitate.

### The cycle that always ends in failure

Then the hesitancy causes the salesman to push a little harder, and in turn the prospect's doubts and suspicions grow a little stronger. As the cycle is repeated in a desperation effort to close the buyer, the sale is lost.

An even greater problem is that each time this occurs the negative selling attitude takes a stronger hold on the real estate man, and, as success breeds success, failure breeds failure.

All the fine selling methods and techniques in the world cannot overcome the handicap of a negative selling attitude. It is the mark of an amateur.

## PSA

Now let's look at his counterpart, the real estate man who wears the Positive Selling Attitude. It is imperative that we have an understanding of this attitude because we *must* adopt it if we are to have any hope of being a top real estate man.

I fervently hope that each of you will find this book a help to climb into the ranks of the high producers in the real estate business, and therefore I urge you to pay particular attention to the meaning intended in this chapter. I mention this because I made the mistake of passing over the "positive selling" aspect of salesmanship for so long. In fact, it was my BIGGEST MISTAKE.

### There is no in-between; you have either NSA or you have PSA

I had read and had been told many times that such a thing existed: I thought it childish, even silly. I associated it with play-acting, self-hypnosis, or some other such nonsense. Don't make that mistake. *It is a very real force.* It is genuine and it is powerful. It is that little difference that will make you a professional and, what's more, it will earn tens of thousands of dollars for you during your career.

PSA also has side benefits. It will relieve a lot of tension and anxiety; it will lessen your workload; it will make you a happier person because you will KNOW you are one of the best, and your income will soar!

Just what is this Positive Selling Attitude? PSA is simply this: everything about you, everything you say and everything you do is RIGHT. AND YOU KNOW IT! The fact that you *know* it and show that you know it is the secret to PSA. Think about that a moment.

The things that make up the cloak of a Positive Selling Attitude I can describe for you, but whether you decide to put it on or not is up to you.

### The three components of a Positive Selling Attitude

1. Be a specialist in your own selected merchandise.
2. Learn new techniques and methods and invent some of your own.
3. Be willing to devote as many hours as necessary, day or night, to do the job properly.

Those are the three main things—the merchandise, the techniques and the time.

However, every bit as important is the multitude of little things. In fact, I might say the little things are even more important. Because of their seeming insignificance, they're often overlooked, but without them there can be no Positive Selling Attitude and you will remain just an average salesman.

Some of the all-important little things are:

*Appearance.* If you leave the house in the morning without looking yourself over critically in a full-length mirror, you are making a grave mistake. It is well said that an untidy person is an untidy salesman. Look your BEST. Buy some new clothes. It would be a great way to start this new approach.

*Frame of mind.* If you wake up with some gripes and complaints, if you are hung over with yesterday's grudges and disappointments, then you must learn to exchange them for pleasantness as you do fresh, clean clothes for soiled ones. This is a matter of getting in tune with the day. Train yourself to think of all the fine people you're going to meet, and all the good things that are going to happen. *To do this is a part of your job.* It is as much a part of your job as listing a home, showing one, or even selling it.

You cannot spend time more profitably than the fifteen minutes or so set aside each morning to brighten up your mental attitude: a quiet time with yourself, or a short bit of inspirational reading, or maybe you're capable simply by force of will of acquiring a pleasant, happy attitude. Whatever is required, it is your obligation to do it. People in other walks of life might be excused from this action, but for those in the real estate business, it is *mandatory.* A smile is a real estate person's "Trust Department."

*Organization.* This is one of the easier ones; it's a matter of deciding what you're going to do, and when you're going to do it, and then doing it. In my case, I start the day with a written list on a shirt-pocket-size card. I wouldn't start the day without it. In a busy man's schedule it is easy to forget something he has planned to do. This will not happen if you check it off a written list. You'll find also you'll get about twice as much done.

*Punctuality.* Remember, if you start the day late, you're late all day. It is far better to eliminate one appointment and be on time for the rest of them than to try to make them all and be late to each one. Punctuality can easily become a habit if you force yourself to practice it for a few days or weeks. A punctual real estate man is a welcome one. This is closely coupled with being organized.

*Be alert.* Those are two golden words that can make you bundles of money. If you do all else asked of you here and are not alert, the rest will be mostly in vain. All day, every day, wherever you go, you will be surrounded by happenings and conversation that can be an invitation to an alert real estate person to do some business. They say the secret to success is to find a need and fill it. In the real estate business we don't need to find it, it's all around us, far more than we can handle. All we need to do is be alert enough to recognize it.

### The origin of creative selling

One test of a professional is his ability to do creative selling. This is done by being alert to opportunity, then thinking of a way to cash in on it. The sale of most property took place in some alert real estate person's mind long before the seller knew he was going to sell or the buyer knew he was going to buy.

*Be a good guy.* A baseball manager once said, "Good guys finish last." Not so in the real estate business. I can think of no one who has more reason to serve the community than those engaged in the real estate business. The better the community and all factions of it, the more active will be the real estate market. If a town is a good town it will grow, and as it does you will get rich. So—serve on community drives, on committees. Express your opinion at town meetings and serve your church and civic organizations. Service is what you're selling, for the most part, but some you must give away. To do so will pay you well. When you become well known you are on the road to success.

*Work.* That word hardly needs to be described. How much work should you do? My answer to that is, how much money do you want to make? As I stated in the opening chapter, the real estate field is studded with hills of gold. They're yours for the working.

A man once asked me if I were told I could have all the silver dollars I could cart away in a day, how much time would I take for lunch? How much would you?

Add to all these practices a few others such as the will to succeed, protecting your good health, a constant attitude of gratitude, a love of your work and, possibly one of the most difficult of all, the willingness to accept the happiness that all this will bring you. Then you pretty much have it made.

### When you believe you have PSA, you have it

In the beginning of the discussion of the positive selling attitude, I said there were a number of things to be done in preparation for adopting this attitude. The remarkable thing is that by attending to the preparation for the goal, you have reached it.

You now have a Positive Selling Attitude. It only remains for you to believe you do. You have it, that is, if you have checked off each of the items above. Difficult? Of course it's difficult. It it were easy, everyone would be doing it.

### Nothing can stop you!

A Positive Selling Attitude will make you a top notch salesman. You know you're good because you *are* good: you know you're right because you *are* right. With this attitude, nothing can stop you! You're on your way to earnings you've never dreamed of! You doubt it? TRY IT! I used it to sell one million dollars worth of real estate in one year!

The next time you are in the presence of a truly top notch real estate man, look him over. Listen to him. Study him carefully. You'll discover that his outstanding characteristic is Positive Selling Attitude. Why not join him? You can, you know. I just told you how.

### Try it—you can always return to mediocrity

At this point the success of your career depends on the decision you make—the decision to put forth the time and effort to acquire a Positive Selling Attitude, or to remain satisfied with your present status. It is true, there is no easy way, there are no success pills, and luck has little if anything to do with it.

At first you will have to put forth a great amount of effort and time. Your biggest problem will be finding the time. I once knew a man who had to set his alarm clock to tell him when to go to bed! It can be done, and YOU can do it. It depends only on how strong your desire is to earn $30,000 or more a year.

If I had to put in a nutshell how I sold a million dollars of real estate in one year, I would say only that I acquired a Positive Selling Attitude. I say to you, adopt this Positive Selling Attitude. We're not talking about small potatoes, you know. We're discussing a way by which you can add up to a QUARTER OF A MILLION DOLLARS MORE to your lifetime earnings!

### Points to remember

1. Your yearly earnings will be no larger than you plan for them to be.
2. A Positive Selling Attitude is the mark of a master salesman.
3. You will make each sale when you have reached the stage where you KNOW you will rather than you HOPE you will.
4. Top notch, high earnings salesmen are nothing more than hard-working average salesmen who have a Positive Selling Attitude.
5. You can earn a QUARTER OF A MILLION DOLLARS MORE in your lifetime with a Positive Selling Attitude.

# CHAPTER 9

# FIVE MAJOR MISTAKES THAT
# LOSE SALES

---

If you are working with qualified buyers and you don't sell them, somewhere you've made a mistake. Let's go over that once more: if you have QUALIFIED buyers and you don't SELL them, somewhere YOU made a MISTAKE. You can't sell a million dollars worth of real estate in one year and make mistakes—at least not many.

How do we know we've made a mistake?

Here's an example: It's the end of the day. You sit dejectedly at your desk. Some of the best prospects you have ever had have just left. You *know* they were buyers. You worked hard with them, but they didn't buy. WHY? Because, SOMEWHERE YOU MADE A MISTAKE.

*When a bona fide buyer meets a true salesman, a sale is inevitable.*

MY RECORDS SHOW THAT DURING MY MILLION DOLLAR YEAR 80% OF MY SALES WERE MADE THE FIRST DAY I MET THE BUYERS!

### FIVE TYPICAL, DEVASTATING MISTAKES

1. You leave the prospects on the doorstep.

You've heard I'm sure that you will make your sale in the first 30 to 60 seconds after you meet your prospects. Nonsense? Not at all.

If you greet your prospects with a sincere smile and a friendly handshake, and bring them inside of yourself to the warmth of your own personality you will indeed make your sale in the first few seconds. I believe that failure to do this is one of the major mistakes that keep many good real estate men from being top salesmen. It might be called "instant friendship." It is the mark of a professional.

2. You assume your prospects know what they want.

After the mutual introduction the real estate man's first question usually is, "What did you people have in mind?"

Then, either well or badly, in few words or many, the prospects relate what they want. It is here the real estate man often makes his second mistake. *He believes them.*

It is appalling to think of the millions of hours wasted every day by real estate people who listen with almost childlike innocence to the inconsistent, incompatible and sometimes impossible requests of their well-meaning prospects. Without qualifying, analyzing or even rationalizing, these men listen and set forth on a course of hopeless action, doomed to almost certain failure. Remember, most buyers are AMATEURS in real estate. YOU are the professional!

3. You listen but don't hear.

Probably the saddest of all mistakes, and the one that undoubtedly causes a great loss of sales is the real estate man's failure to hear. During the average discussion between him and his prospects the prospects reveal time and time again what house they will buy. However, these revelations come in the form of CLUES—many of them, and if only you had been hearing instead of listening, your selling would be over. These clues to what they will buy are dropped without the prospect even realizing it. They must be *heard* by the salesman.

How to recognize these clues is discussed in detail in other chapters. For the moment we are concerned with the mistake of not hearing these clues as they bound past our ears. Learn the difference between listening and hearing. *Listening* is simply waiting for your turn to talk. *Hearing* is awareness of what is being said.

4. The salesman becomes the buyer.

When the prospects are doing most of the talking and gesticulating, and seem to be in charge of the situation, they are selling the salesman. When they insist they must have four bedrooms, must be near a certain school, won't spend over X number of dollars, they are selling the salesman. If he buys all this he's lost. At least his sale is. While they're selling, you're not. There is not time for this nonsense in a million dollar year.

### Buyers often say one thing and do the exact opposite

The many and varied techniques of how to sell run throughout these pages. The topic here is to learn to avoid the mistake of being put in the position of being the buyer. The best way to learn this, so you're not likely to forget, is to experience it one day when your prospects have sold you on the idea that they will only buy a one-story home, close in, and for no more than $20,000. Then you discover, a few days later, that they purchased from your competitor a two-story home, five miles out in the country, for $35,000! You'll have a severe pain in your pocketbook, but you'll remember. After they tell you what they want then you decide what they will buy. Often there is a vast difference.

5. The over-sell.

The fifth of the major mistakes is the over-sell and its equally nonproductive counterpart, the under-sell.

In every instance there comes the psychological moment to close your sale. If you let that moment pass—if you keep right on selling—you are guilty of over-sell and you are finished. You must learn to watch for that psychological moment, for it may come early or late; in the house; in your car; in the office; most any place. When it comes, STOP! Your selling is over. Write up your deal and go home. If you over-sell you will unsell. Continue your conversation only after the sales agreement is SIGNED!

### Under-sell is a twin to over-sell

The mistake of the over-sell is most often committed by the go-go, fireball type of real estate man who hasn't learned to pace himself. Its opposite, the under-sell, is usually a mistake made by the quiet, reserved type of real estate man who is usually behind the sale instead of ahead of it. Under-sell happens when the salesman has done a complete, neat, and tidy job of selling. He has selected the right house, answered all the questions, settled the financing matters, brought the prospects to the spot marked "X." But then he commits the fatal mistake. He fails to ask them if they want to buy the house. Until he does, usually they won't.

I wish I had a dollar for each and every time a sale has been lost because the salesman neglected to ask,

"Would you like to buy this house?"

Whether it's a case of going too far or not far enough—overselling or under-selling—it's a mistake. Top-producing real estate people do neither.

### A very important decision you must face

Here is the opportunity to increase your income six, eight, up to ten thousand dollars a year. Eliminate these mistakes and watch what happens. The trouble is, you probably will give no thought to the fact that if the shoe fits, you should do something about it. However, maybe with you it will be different. Maybe you are the one who will take the time, and put forth the effort to become a top producer and earn $30,000 to $50,000 a year.

If you will correct the five major mistakes most real estate men make you will not only find yourself in a high income bracket, but you will be amazed to realize that you're putting forth far less effort than before. You're now being alert and vigilant; you are hearing instead of listening; you are using your knowledge to SELL.

If you will then check yourself for correction of a few minor mistakes, you will become a polished professional and the high caliber of your career will be assured for as long as you choose to stay in the real estate business.

## SMALL MISTAKES THAT LOSE BIG COMMISSIONS

You will also lose sales if:
- —You are a late starter.
- —You are not thoroughly acquainted with your merchandise.
- —You jump to conclusions.
- —You do not plan your day.
- —You become a "dollar salesman."

### I learned it was a mistake to be a late starter

Of the many parts that it takes to make up a million-dollar salesman I can think of none higher in my estimation than being an early starter. I learned that an hour in the freshness and quiet of the early morning was easily worth two or three later in the day. One of the problems in working up from an average to the top salesman is having enough time, so an hour added to your day is invaluable. By coming in early I found that I was tuned and waiting to meet the activities of the day, instead of being late and never quite catching up. I used the extra hour to review the preceding day's activities and to fully acquaint myself with new listings, sales made, price changes, and so forth, which are constantly occurring. But, most important of all, I used this time to plan my day.

### Your merchandise is HOMES, Not HOUSES

Often you will hear real estate people make reference to "buildings" or "houses." They are out of tune with what selling residential real estate is all about. We are selling *homes,* in every poetic, romantic sense of the word. As it is said, a man's home is his castle. It's here he knows happiness and sadness; it's where his family is born, and some of them die. It's where he lives. You can't call this a building or a house: it's his home, and the quicker you learn to feel this way about it, the quicker you will always have the very best homes to sell at your fingertips. It is part of the "attitude" you must develop.

### The qualities that will sell are sensed, not seen

To acquire the merchandise that *you* are going to sell, you must visit every listing, but you don't "look" or "inspect," you *feel* the qualities the homes contain. Warmth, cleanliness, beauty, cheerfulness, friendliness, hominess are not made out of bricks and mortar, paint or lumber. These are the qualities that sell. Some houses have them—some don't. If you *feel* them in a home, put it on your list. It's half sold. Experience has taught me that quaintness will outsell quality: charm will outsell convenience; and a good feeling will outsell a good floor plan.

Know your merchandise—yes! But select for your special list the houses that you *feel* will sell. If you follow this method you will have twice the fun and four times the income.

### I learned it was a mistake to jump to conclusions

Jumping to conclusions was my favorite sport, until I learned it was costing me sales. False assumptions and "selling myself" were other forms of jumping to conclusions that I allowed to strangle my career. These sales killers crop up in many forms: for one thing, I cut short the qualifying step, to discover many wasted hours later that I was working with buyers who were ready and willing but not able to buy. Frequently, I sold myself on the belief that what they said they wanted was indeed what they really wanted. In letting this belief influence me I allowed the buyers to "sell me" and therefore I could not sell them. It was difficult for me to accept the often-heard phrase, "All buyers are liars," until it was explained that it is sort of a game buyers play, and making evasive statements is their method of self-defense, and perfectly allowable. The answer is to "think," "analyze," and *then* act.

### Plan your work and work your plan is old but wise advice

This is how I did it: each morning I listed on a three by five index card the things that I intended to do that day. I seldom, if ever, accomplished what was on the list, but the important thing was that I made it and I worked at it. Some of the things I had on the card were prospects I wanted to call, houses I wanted to check, listings I wanted to ask for, reading I wanted to do, people I wanted to visit. I made the list long, with the most pressing things first. There was a time when I thought this was amateurish and unnecessary, but I was wrong. It gave me control of my work.

There was one other thing that was very important to me, and started my day off with an excellent mental attitude. During this extra hour I wrote at least one thank-you note. Some time during the previous day I would have been treated to some kind or thoughtful act, and however large or small it was, I would make a mental note to send the doer a note of thanks the following morning. I can't speak for the recipients, but I know, for me, it was a mental vitamin tablet. Having cleared up any details left over from the day before, when the magical hour of nine o'clock rolled around, and the banks, savings and loans, lawyers, city officials, title companies and other real estate offices opened their doors, I was in control of myself, I was in control of the day, I was indeed ready for business. I have little doubt that without this added hour my first big year would never have materialized. How much better to be waiting for business to come to you than to be frantically chasing after it!

### Serving your clients must be
### more important than earning dollars

In a business where we delve deeply into the lives and welfare of so many people, if we believe we do not need to discuss such philosophies as honesty and integrity we are surely kidding ourselves. Should we become "dollar salesmen" and concern ourselves only with earning a commission, then we are parasites to the real estate profession. Furthermore, if we continue this policy, the commissions will become increasingly more difficult to earn and our careers will soon be ended. Why this is I don't know, but I do know that it's true.

If we let ourselves or our careers become more important than the welfare of our clients, then we *are* "dollar salesmen." If we don't, the dollars will take care of themselves—literally thousands of them. It was one of the strange and amazing things I learned in my year of a million dollars in sales. I can think of no greater mistake that you can make than to overlook or ignore your assigned role in the lives of the people that you serve. It is a role dictated by prestige, earned by thousands of your predecessors in the real estate profession.

### The many roles of a real estate man

Consider for a moment the power and influence you have. You advise, guide, and direct the people who come to you in confidence concerning the buying or selling of a home, a matter that involves thousands upon thousands of dollars; dollars that often represent the savings of a man's lifetime. Sometimes you are the advisor to a widow, or to innocent young newlyweds who are going to plunge deeply into debt. If you advise them carelessly, without diligent consideration to their needs, desires and capabilities simply to earn a quick commission, the result to your clients could be devastating, if not tragic. The golden rule must have been written for those of us in the real estate business.

I believe the real estate profession is granted a privilege denied other salesmen of the world, because for a little while we are permitted to become a part of the lives of the people we deal with. We become their friend, their confidant, their advisor. They often share intimate problems; ask our help and opinion as they would an old and trusted friend. In a sense, they place in our hands a signed check, and trust us to spend it wisely on a home for them.

You will know success in the fullest sense of the word if you can genuinely be what they believe you are—a person to be trusted.

### The Golden Rules of selling real estate

I think as good a rule to follow as I ever heard is: Never sell a house that you wouldn't be willing to buy yourself if you were in the same circumstances as your prospect.

Another Golden Rule of selling that I have found completely dependable, disregarding for a moment the moral aspect of it, is: *Good, old-fashioned honesty will put more money in a salesman's pocket than any other thing he can use.* If you will remember to put your client's welfare first, and the importance of your sale second, word-of-mouth recognition in your community will soon make you the best known and the richest real estate person around!

It is one of my most cherished thoughts that I could drop by for a visit and a cup of coffee with any of the families to whom I ever sold a house, and be welcome. That sort of reward may not be spendable—but that's what's so nice about it.

### Examples of mistakes I corrected

One of the experiences that taught me the value of not jumping to conclusions came about one dismal day. Returning to the office with my prospects, I felt utter defeat. I had shown them every home listed in our office which even came close to what they said they wanted, to no avail. As I was trying to arrange an appointment with them for the following day, my sales manager, who had been present during the qualifying period earlier in the day, handed me a slip of paper which said, "Show them the Johnson property on Maple Avenue."

My reaction was extreme irritation. The property on Maple Avenue in no way or manner fulfilled their stated requirements: in fact, it was almost entirely opposite to everything they said they wanted. But, I asked my buyers if they would take the time to look at one more property. They agreed and, to my astonishment, bought the house on the spot. When I asked the sales manager what had told her that they would buy this particular house, her answer was, "Fifteen years of experience." It was in this manner that I learned that I was obviously making some very big mistakes. However, I didn't intend to wait fifteen years to learn how to correct them.

**A case in point.** First, I knew *now* that buyers, either intentionally or not, do not tell the entire truth. Second, there had to have been a clue which I had missed. It was apparent that one word, one look, or one thing about them spoke out loud and clear. I was so busy *listening* to them sell me that I didn't *hear* it. The sales manager did. Try as I might, I was never able to discover that particular tip-off clue. All I knew was that there was one, and I had missed it. It was at this time that I stopped jumping to conclusions and quit making quick assumptions. I set out to sell the buyers rather than letting them sell me.

**The tip-off clue.** The day soon came when I had the chance to exercise my newfound wariness on my own. One busy Saturday morning a lady was ushered to my desk. After we introduced ourselves she became quite serious and said, "Mr. Gardiner, I am looking for . . . ." And she proceeded to describe the size, location and price of property she would be interested in buying. She talked at great length, and I listened intently. I said, "I think we have two or three properties you'd be interested in," but as I reached for my listing book, I suddenly realized that she had done a wonderful job of selling *me*. The warning device in my mind signalled frantically. The one thing about which she was emphatic, *and* the only stipulation she repeated, was that the house *must* be in a quiet neighborhood. This emphasis, coupled with the information that she did not drive and that she would often be visiting her sister in a neighboring town, stimulated me to try my first case of applied sales psychology.

**The first test of a new technique.** I reasoned that because of the weeks and sometimes months of inclement weather in our area she would benefit by living close to the train station or to a main high-way with bus service. Of course, in either event she would have considerable noise to contend with. *She realized all of this.* How-ever, if she could convince me to try to solve this problem—get her into a quiet neighborhood and still keep her close to transportation —fine. She was perfectly willing to let me wrestle with this formid-able, if not impossible, task. I became excited: if my reasoning was correct I had discovered a buyer's quirk which would save me hours of needless work with future prospects. By telling me what they *wouldn't* buy, they had told me the very thing they *would* buy!

We had a comfortable, two-bedroom home listed at a good price but located less than 200 feet from the main highway which ran through the town. However, the interurban bus stopped every hour at the corner. I showed my prospect this property, using as my single selling point the nearness of the bus stop and its hourly schedule. After a thorough inspection, but without one word of objection to its location, she bought the house.

**The folly of indulging impossible requests.** Subsequent incidents proved that I had uncovered one of my greatest mistakes. Allowing myself to be caught up and carried away by the lengthy descriptions and incompatible desires eagerly expressed by my buyers was a *mistake.* I only compounded the problem by foolishly encouraging them to think that I could and would magically produce a nonexis-tent home. They wanted dream homes, looked for castles in the air; and I wasted untold hours indulging their fantasies. From then on, I no longer listened naively to demands presented to me, when a little common sense and calm analysis indicated they were im-possible.

An indisputable confirmation of this discovery occurred the day a young executive and his wife presented me with two handwritten sheets of requirements for a home, among which were that it have four bedrooms and be in a top neighborhood. After I had read them the husband said complacently, "As you can see, we've given considerable thought to the details of the house we want. We're in no hurry, and intend to look until we find just such a house." His next sentence told me the type of house to show them: "You'll notice the first item on my wife's list is a one-story house, and that I've set the maximum price at $22,000. Now we're in your hands." There was the familiar tip-off. He had repeated two items on the list. In doing so he emphasized a combination he *knew* was highly improbable to find.

**The over-emphasis indicated an easy compromise.** Less than two hours later they had willingly, even eagerly, purchased a two-story residence for $27,500. In times past I would have shown them many houses, each filling a few of their needs, but it would have been a fruitless day, and by evening we would all have been tired, confused, perplexed and disappointed. Because they were reasonable people, it wasn't hard to make them see that they would have to compromise in order to have most of the items each of them wanted. It wasn't hard—because they already knew it.

**A little clear thinking saves many wasted hours.** To get the square footage and the necessary four bedrooms into a one-floor plan house would have made the cost prohibitive, and to have a home in a neighborhood in keeping with the husband's position, even a two-story home, called for a higher price than their stated limit. I showed them a large, two-story redwood home on a beautiful wooded lot, in an excellent but not prestige neighborhood, and their problem and mine was solved. Analyzing rather than believing what the prospects said proved to reduce the time needed to make a sale by 75 percent. I had learned to watch for a tip-off clue. They never failed to come.

### The affliction of procrastination

Procrastination was so common with me in my daily routine that I hardly noticed I was guilty of it. It was inevitable that sooner or later I would have to do battle with this deadly sales killer. The "sooner" came in a traumatic manner. I had often heard my sales manager say that a lesson was well learned when it hit you in your pocketbook, and that's the way it happened.

**The high cost of a delayed phone call.** The procrastination occurred one evening when I put off making a phone call: humiliation followed the next morning when I did.

A large and lovely home came on the market one afternoon, and I felt sure that I had some prospects who would buy it. As evening approached, I sat at my desk debating whether or not to call them. Finally, because I was tired, or because I wanted to watch a certain television program, or maybe because I was just an habitual procrastinator, I decided to wait until the following morning. When I did call, I was literally staggered to find that a competitor had called the night before, showed them the house, and they bought it. A commission of more than $2,000 went out the window because of my negligence, and this brought me face to face with the presence of this excessively bad habit. It made me painfully conscious that I could hold out little hope for success, unless I could find a way to eliminate procrastination.

**Diligence for a dime.**—But I did find it. As the pain to pride and pocketbook began to wear off, I reviewed my working habits diligently looking for the answer. But the days passed and I realized that the old habit of putting off till later still plagued me. Then one afternoon as I walked by a variety store I saw a display of motto cards. One of them leaped out at me. It said, "DO IT NOW!" There was the answer. Simple, undeniable, and only a dime. I bought it and promptly taped the card to the prospect index box on my desk. I added at the bottom of the card, in red pencil, the name of the prospects whom I had lost through procrastination. This constant reminder did the trick and the habit was soon broken. A simple thing, maybe even silly, but that ten cent card made me a whale of a lot of money!

### The folly of "follow through"

One of the many things I was told when I first went into the real estate business was that a salesman's middle name should be "follow through." This appeared to be wise advice. I liked the sound of it. I adopted it, used it consistently, and in doing so *lost* more sales than I care to recall! Again, it was a matter of learning the hard way. Blessed is he who learns hard but learns well. If you'll examine this phenomenon with me a moment you may, as I did, add a few more sales to the year's total. And, after all, that's what this is all about.

**A job half done is no job at all.** A lawyer friend of mine telephoned me one day to say that some clients of his were in the market for an expensive home. He gave me all the information I could possibly need. I had been given a good lead and now, since my middle name was supposed to be "follow through," follow through I did. First I called them on the telephone, introduced myself, engaged them in friendly conversation, and told them I would send out some information on a few of our select homes. I promptly composed a letter describing in detail a number of fine properties. When the letter was in the outgoing mail basket, I sat back in my chair and basked in the thoroughness of my excellent "follow through." I thought in a few days they would contact me, eager to buy a home.

A day or so later, in a subsequent conversation with the lawyer, he needled me for not having sold his clients a house after he had given me a jump on my competitors. It seems that a saleslady in a neighboring office had learned about the same prospects from her hairdresser. I made the "follow through." She made the sale.

**Go where the action is.** This incident called for further study to be sure a lost sale of this nature did not happen again. To control the matter in the future I had to review the past, and I recalled an amazing number of cases where my "follow through" had been well done, but produced no sale. It wasn't difficult to conclude that I must from now on follow through on the "follow through." I believe that the theory of "follow through," which is preached to all salesmen, works like a sort of anesthesia. It creates the feeling of having done a good job, and by that very fact loses sales. You feel confident that you have set in motion factors which will produce a sale, when in reality you have been lured into complacency with this inaccurate single-phase theory. The execution of the all-important second phase is a fairly obvious procedure. After the "follow through" you simply go where the action is—*go* to your buyer, and *stay* with him until he buys.


## IT'S A MISTAKE TO BE A
## LIGHT-SWITCH REAL ESTATE MAN

The "light-switch real estate man" is the one who quits at a precise time each day. For success in the real estate business this simply can't be!

*If you turn off your mind with the office lights,*
*you will miss sales*

Businessmen throughout the nation are advised to leave their work at the office. I insist that this cannot apply to the real estate business. In the days when I turned off my mind with the office lights I unquestionably missed sales. The mind, if permitted uninterrupted continuity, will function like an unattended computer, fitting, checking, placing bits and pieces of information acquired during the hurly-burly day and, finally, with the precision of a perfect machine, will deliver to you the exact steps with which to solve a problem or consummate a sale. The answer to many a problem involved with putting together a deal came to me when I was relaxing at home and even, on some occasions, as I slept. More than once my nocturnal computer matched a buyer with a house which I turned into a sale the next day.

### Adjust your time to the public's convenience

In my low production years I was unwilling to sacrifice my evenings, social activities and entertainment opportunities: in short, I was not willing to pay the price to be successful. My desire for success, however, did not lessen, and I realized that this had to be made compatible with the facts. The facts were plain and simple: I must adjust my time to that of the buying public.

### Trade slow hours for productive ones

Most people were busy during the daylight hours earning a living. When I adjusted my time to theirs I quickly learned that the golden hours for making sales were evenings and weekends. I cannot visualize anyone engaged in the business of selling residential real estate having more than mediocre success without adopting this extension of the work day. The rapid increase in sales for anyone who does will compensate him well. In my case, I became able and willing to accept this rigorous routine by making some perfectly logical modifications. I took some leisure hours during the day.

### Places and ways to unwind

If my work schedule permitted, I took an extended lunch hour. Once in a while I would go to my home and after lunch take a revitalizing nap. If this couldn't be arranged, very often I would stop in at the City Library during the afternoon, where enjoyment of peace and quiet and endlessly good reading for an hour or so left me rested and rejuvenated for the evening's work. I also fondly remember visiting a certain quiet place regularly, where I shed my tensions, unwound my nerves, and gathered the strength and serenity that served me well until the day ended. There was an arboretum in our area, open to the public, and it was there I found my quiet place, beneath a stately tree or beside a duck-dotted pond. I hope you are so fortunate.

### The second half of your day starts in the evening

Successful selling techniques are wonderful things to have, but first you must find the opportunities and the proper time to apply them. The after-dinner hours provide that time. I have kept a record of the dates my sales were made; I've often wished that I had recorded the hour. I wouldn't be surprised if 50 percent of them were made after six o'clock in the evening.

**Reaching for the top.** By correcting most of my mistakes, by adjusting my hours to peak sales periods, and by applying my newly developed sales techniques, I had arrived at a plateau that would guarantee me an income well above the average. I now reached for those extra sales which would put me in the top income bracket. The "extra sales" were there, they are always there, but I had to be alert and be willing to leave the beaten path to find them.

**A desperate buyer doesn't stop house-hunting at sundown.** Have you noticed how the world changes after nine o'clock at night? Stores and offices close, lights go out, traffic thins, and all business is abandoned until dawn. Should there be, as there often is, a single buyer who, in one or another degree of desperation, is still driving the streets searching for a home, and should your services be available to him, you have an anxious buyer. If he is handled properly, it is an almost certain sale. I have experienced this many times.

**You can sell a house today up to midnight tonight.** I fondly recall one instance of nocturnal buyers. The people came into the office shortly before ten o'clock in the evening. They were weary, wary, and a little apologetic. They explained their urgency: the husband had been transferred from another state, and the wife had been able to make arrangements to join her husband for only one week to assist in the house hunting. The time was running out, and the wife had to return home the following afternoon. They had left the office of one of my competitors a little earlier, they said, when the salesman suggested that they postpone their search until the following day. Within a few minutes I had arranged three appointments.

Incidentally, I have no qualms about making late appointments with sellers, since I feel that if I am willing to work diligently to sell their home, the least they can do is to cooperate by permitting me to show it. If they are really interested in selling their home, they seldom refuse. In this instance the third house on the list delighted my buyers and, after they had inspected it extensively, I had no difficulty in getting their signature on an offer to purchase contract. They left, happy and excited. I felt the glow that one experiences with a signed contract in his possession. As I reached for the switch to turn off the office lights, I glanced at the wall clock. The hands pointed at midnight.

By now, a reasonable facsimile of the above-average real estate man had begun to emerge. I had isolated some major mistakes, and corrected them. To maintain this status, I prepared for myself a list of points to remember:

1. If you start the day late, you're late all day.
2. Don't jump to conclusions. Don't assume things are what they seem to be.
3. Procrastination is not to be tolerated.
4. Remember the all-important second phase of the "follow through."
5. If you're going to reach for the moon, you have to work at night.

CHAPTER 10

# TWO SIMPLE FORMULAS
# THAT WORK LIKE MAGIC

---

Formulas differ from techniques in that a formula is a precise and specific method of performance and a technique is a variable guide to performance.

The formulas relating to matters of real estate as discussed here fulfill this description to the letter.

### THE MATHEMAGICS FORMULA THAT
### CHANGES RENTERS INTO BUYERS

Quite often genuine buyers came into the office in the guise of renters. They were seeking information, feeling out the market, from the protection of their renter classification. No magic formula was needed to convert this type of prospect—he was already a buyer, and needed only to find a real estate person whom he felt he could trust. He would then readily buy.

*A renter is often a buyer if*
*you look under the surface*

It is an entirely different matter with the renter who is afraid to buy, or, who really believes it's cheaper to rent, or who just has never given much thought to becoming a homeowner. However, this kind of a renter can also often be converted into a buyer. I discovered this by following my determination not to overlook any possibility in my quest for a million dollars in sales in one year. I devised my MATHEMAGICS formula and added at least $150,-000 to my year's sales.

Whenever I heard a prospect say, "We're looking for a rental," I used the MATHEMAGICS formula on them, and the odds were in my favor that I would make a sale.

### Using the formula that changes renters into buyers

For some time after I entered the real estate business I treated inquiries for rentals as I had seen the other salesmen do. I would politely tell the callers that I knew of nothing to rent and that I would be glad to take their names and call them if anything came in. I would dispose of them as quickly as possible by suggesting that they watch the "Houses for Rent" column in the newspapers. Then one day I watched my sales manager perform a bit of magic.

### The two types of renters who are rich sources for sales

An inquiry on rentals came to her attention and I saw her, very professionally, change renters into buyers. She made a sale and earned a very nice commission. I would have sent these people on their way. What a shock this was to me! I was searching for ways to make more sales, and here I discover I had actually been running buyers out the door! So, it was off in a corner for a talk with myself about this.

I decided if there were various types of buyers, then there must be various types of renters. A study indicated that some would rent because they could not afford to buy, some because they simply didn't want the responsibility of owning a home. Others rented while they looked for a home to buy, and still others fully intended to buy a home, but always next year: this year they were going to rent. Obviously, the last two were rich sources for additional sales.

### The three steps to convert renters to buyers

A plan for cultivating this field had to be devised. Special qualifying methods were needed. Once I had determined that a renter was a potential buyer I would need a bold plan, strong with conviction, designed to create interest and desire. It must appeal to the inherent desire of all wives to own a home, but even more important, it must dramatically convince the husband that it would save him thousands of dollars. I devised a plan with three steps:

1. Qualification to determine if a sale were possible. If they are able to buy, then your job is to make them ready and willing.

2. Winning the wife. Rare indeed is the woman who will not succumb to a picturesque description of shade trees, rose gardens, bright kitchens and an abundance of closet space. Her eyes will sparkle, her entire attitude will be eager, and she will readily admit she would just love to have her own home rather than rent.

3. Explaining the economic factor to the husband. A home is one of the few commodities that you can buy, use for years then sell it for as much as or more than you paid for it! Rent money is gone forever.

### The "Mathemagics" formula

Monthly rent $\times$ 12 $\times$ 20 years = 240 rent receipts

Or, converted into dollars, using $150 as the average rental, and 20 years as the time factor—

$$\$150 \times 12 = \$1,800 \times 20 = \$36,000$$

THIRTY-SIX THOUSAND DOLLARS given to landlords— enough to buy TWO houses.

### A lesson in simple economics also

If this astonishing bit of mathematics didn't discourage the prospects from renting a home, I would give them a further lesson in economics by explaining that purchasing a home was a form of enforced savings. When they bought a home, I told them, they were not spending their money, they were investing it. They were simply taking their money from one place and putting it in another.

The equity in the home grew each month. At income tax time, the year's interest and taxes were totally deductible. Other factors that helped to convince them were: market appreciation, security, credit rating, independence, and pride of ownership. I pointed out to them that homes, like diamonds, could be purchased, used, and then sold for as much as, or more than, the original purchase price. I concluded my arguments by asking them, "Why should you buy a house for your landlord? Buy one for yourself."

This formula was very effective because it worked quickly. I either uncovered a buyer, or I didn't. It added a few extra sales to my million dollar year.

### How one idea for selling was born

Incidentally, the concluding question mentioned above, which really gets results, came to my mind one afternoon while I was searching for a clinching statement to convince a couple to buy rather than to rent. They were interesting people, probably a little past middle age; hard-working, solid citizens. It was a rather dreary day—rain had set in in the morning, with all indications of continuing throughout the day. Business was slow, and when the couple came in the office inquiring for a rental, I decided to do my best to convert them to buyers. I went through my three-step plan in my best manner: they didn't convert. I went through it again. Still nothing. Finally the wife clarified matters by saying, "Mr. Gardiner, every so often I go through this searching for another place to rent with my husband because he gets angry for one reason or another with our landlord. We have been renting the top floor of a duplex for almost twenty years. Whenever we have words with the landlord, who lives below us, my husband says we're going to move out, but we never do."

I looked at the husband and said, *"You* have paid for the house; why don't you tell him to move out?" I continued, "Of course, you can't tell him that because, even though you *have* paid for it, the deed is in his name. The point is, why should you buy a house for your landlord? Why don't you buy one for yourself?" That did it. I had a convert, a buyer.

The little twist to this story that always delighted me was that I sold him a duplex and now he's letting someone buy a house for him.

## THE "IF I—WILL YOU" FORMULA
## THAT PRODUCES ASTONISHING RESULTS

When the odds are overwhelmingly against him, it seems only right that a real estate man should have one formula that works like a magic wand. He has so much to do, and so little time to do it. His prospects may discuss purchasing a home for six months or a year: when they walk in the office the real estate man, if he's lucky, may have fifteen minutes to probe the depth of their personalities, draw out their likes and dislikes, win their confidence, and select two or three homes most likely to please them.

### The complex obligations of those marketing real estate

To compound his problems, he must counteract the erroneous advice of friends and relatives; out-think and out-work his competitors; determine when his prospects are telling the truth and when they're not; engage in verbal fencing matches with sellers to prevent them from saying the wrong things in the presence of his buyers; push aside the unreasonable and unreal fears of the buyers which prevent them from committing in writing an agreement to buy; and engage in mental combat to convince the buyer the house is worth more than he's offering, and to convince the seller that it's worth less than he's asking.

In fact, no one believes more than I do that real estate people throughout this country perform brilliant feats of salesmanship, daily, in the face of tremendous odds unknown in other professions. It is just not right, when they've done their job so diligently, to have their efforts stymied by a single objection from their prospects. If there is an all-conquering technique, a magic wand of selling, if you will, then every real estate person should have it. Anyone expecting to sell a million dollars in one year MUST have it.

There is such a technique. I call it the "Double I—Double U—Y."

### The most versatile technique of them all

This remarkable, sales-clinching, unassailable method is called "If I—Will You." Here's how it works:

You have found the home that fills the bill and you are pressing for a closing. The direct, point-blank question is always the best way to do this, so you ask,

"Would you like to buy this home?" or "Shall I draw up the agreement?"

The following are a few of your prospects' various answers and your responses,

(*Prospect*): "We like this home very much, but the interior badly needs repainting."

(*You*): "IF I can get the home redecorated, WILL YOU buy it?"

(*Prospect*): "We think this home is at least a thousand dollars too high."

(*You*): "IF I can get the owners down a thousand dollars, WILL YOU buy it?"

(*Prospect*): "We feel the laundry and kitchen appliances should go with the house."

(*You*): "IF I can convince the owners to leave the washer and dryer, stove and refrigerator, WILL YOU buy the house?"

(*Prospect*): "We really prefer a new home like this, but after we make our down payment, we won't have money left for drapes and carpeting."

(*You*): "IF I can get the builder to install drapes and carpeting, WILL YOU buy the house?"

(*Prospect*): "We both really love this home, but it's so far from shopping, and we only have one car."

(*You*): "IF I can arrange for an inexpensive second car for your wife to go with the property, WILL YOU buy the home?"

(*Prospect*): "The down payment you quoted is a little more than we can handle."

(*You*): "IF I can prevail upon the owners to take back a second mortgage, WILL YOU buy the house?"

### The limitless use of this formula

As you can see, the application is almost endless. There are very few objections that can't be fielded with the "If I—Will You." Your buyer likes the property, but:

The driveway is in bad shape.
IF I have the driveway repaired, WILL YOU . . .

The carpeting is soiled.
IF I arrange for the carpeting to be cleaned, WILL YOU . . .

The roof has some bad spots.

IF I have those spots repaired, WILL YOU . . .

and on and on and on.

"IF I—WILL YOU" are powerful words, magic words, words that will add thousands of dollars to your income. They work like magic because they remove your buyer's objections and call his bluff, so to speak. By removing his objection, you have put it squarely up to him, and he will be faced with the fact that he can't very readily say anything but . . . yes, he will buy the house, after you have removed the reason why he wouldn't. What else can he do?

Sometimes there are multiple objections. If so, remove them one by one with the "IF I—WILL YOU" method. It is the most productive technique that I ever used. Take it and use it: it is one of the main keys to the MILLION DOLLAR CLUB.

### Points to Remember

1. If qualification shows them able to buy, then they must be made ready and willing.
2. Apply the formula of "Mathemagics."
3. Renters are paying for a house they'll never own.
4. The "If I—Will You" technique is almost infallible. It is the Master Key to the Million Dollar Club.

CHAPTER **11**

# THE ADVANTAGES OF BOW-AND-
# ARROW OVER SHOTGUN SELLING

To SELL $1,000,000 WORTH OF RESIDENTIAL REAL ESTATE in one year will require an average of one sale a week and will then earn for the real estate man commissions approximating $30,000! If this is your goal, and there's no reason why not, then you simply cannot waste time shooting at your sales with a shotgun without aim or purpose—that is, figuratively speaking, throwing a great number of houses at your prospects like pellets from a shotgun, and hoping that one will reach the bull's-eye.

Instead, a technique is required that hits HARD. FAST, and DEAD ON THE MARK. I developed such a technique. It's called the BOW-AND-ARROW method! It will let you zero in on the house you will sell, *before* you leave the office.

### THE STORY OF JIM,
### THE SHOTGUN SALESMAN

Jim taught me in one day the futility of selling real estate with the shotgun method. He believed that if he showed enough houses the odds were favorable that he would sell one. He was busy, but his sales were few.

Jim knew his merchandise well, and there was no question that on this particular day Jim's prospects were buyers. But he chose to forego the probing for clues that would have pointed to the exact house they would have bought. Instead, armed with a listing book and a pocketful of keys, they toured the town on a search that would take up most of the day, and could only cause the buyers to lose their perspective, become confused, and be considerably further from purchasing a home than they were in the beginning. Jim was engaged in selling houses to people, rather than people to houses—in other words, he was shotgun selling.

### When a promise is an apology

He returned to the office during the day to pick up more keys and make a phone call; then he was off again, crisscrossing the town, showing house after house in the blind hope that the next one would be "it." As the day wore on, Jim's supply of houses ran low and as evening settled he showed the last one, to no avail. He left his buyers with the promise, "I'll call you when something comes in," which is not a *promise* at all, but an *apology*.

### Buyers buy only one home—the right one

Jim was disappointed and defeated, but what is deplorable, he was deceived. Deceived by himself for failing to search for the clues that would send him straight as an arrow to the house they would buy—in fact, to the house they *did* buy the following morning through a salesman from another office. *Jim had this house among his listings.* It appears he showed all of his houses but one—the RIGHT one.

I was deeply affected by this wholesale waste of time and the ultimate loss to Jim of what should have been a quick and easy sale. A better method had to be found.

A review of the situation revealed what Jim had learned during the qualifying period, as well as what he had not learned.

*What Jim learned*
1. The name of his prospects
   (Mr. and Mrs. Radcliffe)
2. The size of the home they were seeking
   (Three bedrooms, basement and garage)
3. The price they expected to pay
   (Around $25,000)

*What Jim COULD HAVE learned*

Through *general* questions:

1. Why they were buying

   (Moving from another city or state: income justified a better home: family was growing and they needed a larger home: family shrinking, needed a smaller home: had rented for years and now had sufficient cash to buy: newly married)

2. The style they preferred

   (Cape Cod, Georgian, colonial, multi-level, ranch, contemporary, etc.)

3. Was there a reason for the $25,000 limit?

   (Would they and *could* they pay $30,000 or $35,000 if they had to, to get the house they wanted?)

4. The number of children

   (If there were children, how would their ages, number and desires affect the sale?)

5. Their preference of exterior construction

   (Brick, frame, or other)

Through *probing* questions:

6. The style, size and price of their last home

   (And a little encouragement would get them to describe homes of friends or relatives that particularly appealed to them)

7. Did they entertain frequently?

   (If so, a recreation or activity room, as well as a formal dining room, would probably be one of their unspoken desires. Also, a large, attractive lawn for social gatherings and games would be a selling factor.)

8. What were the family hobbies?

   (An avid golfer would vote heavily in favor of a home near the golf course: a family that enjoyed swimming would be attracted to a home with a pool, or one near a community pool: gardeners would be delighted with large flower beds, rose gardens, and even a small greenhouse.)

9. What style of furniture did they own?

   (Tastes in furniture reflect tastes in architecture.)

The answer to the first of these questions would have given Jim a general idea of the homes to show the Radcliffes; and, in this particular case, the answer to the last one would have targeted him in on THE house they were most likely to buy.

### The tip-off clue was the style of the buyer's furniture

During the series of probing questions Jim would have learned that the Radcliffes had a houseful of very fine Early American furniture in storage. He would have shown them the one house he missed, which was a Cape Cod, with wooden shutters on the windows, a fireplace of Early American design, wainscoting in the dining room, and a living room partially panelled in knotty cedar. In other words the home was made to order for the Radcliffe's prized furnishings.

Instead of spending eight hours showing a dozen or more houses, without making a sale, he would have spent a little while probing for clues, then shown *one* house and earned for himself and his office a commission of nearly $2,000, as his competitor did the following day.

## HOW THE BOW-AND-ARROW METHOD WORKS

I came to realize that:
1. People buy with their hearts, not their heads.
    a. Therefore, find the hidden desire that touches their heart-strings.
2. The INNER man buys the house.
    a. Find, by probing questions, what the inner man *wants*.
3. You must learn these things *before* you leave the office.
    a. Look for the target; then you'll *know* what house to show your prospects instead of *guessing*.

### Selecting target homes

Since we are discussing selling people to houses rather than houses to people, by the bow-and-arrow method, it is necessary to understand that first we must select target homes. It is very important to remember that I picked homes with features that were sufficiently unique, in my opinion, to make them a target home, and I picked them from homes that I had *already* selected as being in the top 10 percent of the listed properties. The top 10 percent refers to the condition, price and desirability of all the homes available on the market. A target home is one of the homes among the TOP 10 PERCENT of the listings, but which has one or more unusual or unique feature that will make it PARTICULARLY SPECIAL to someone.

### Target homes are chosen from your selected listings

For the bow-and-arrow method to work to its full efficiency it is mandatory for you to memorize the feature that makes a particular home a target home, so that during a future interview or qualifying period, when a totally unexpected clue is dropped, you can instantly match it with the target homes. It requires an alert attitude. My target homes in each price category were a part of, but kept separate from, my selected listings.

### If the clue fits

If you can't rely on your memory, I suggest indexing alphabetically the features that you consider unique, giving the address of the house and other pertinent data, so that when a clue is dropped you may refer to the index quickly, select the home that fits the clue, and proceed with the sale. A small 3 x 5 looseleaf book with alphabetized tabs should do.

There are as many features as there are stars in the heavens which would raise a *good* home to a *unique and highly desirable target property* in someone's eyes. An alert and knowledgeable real estate man recognizes some of these as:

artistically designed flower gardens
air conditioning
a hideaway room
a dormitory bedroom
two or more fireplaces
a music room

a colonnaded entrance
a slate roof with copper gutters
a wooded lot with a small stream
a corral with a stable
a spiral staircase
stained glass windows

a sunken tub in the bath
cathedral ceilings with exposed
    beams
a screened porch
inside-outside thermostatically
    controlled heating plant
bay windows
a self-contained guest house
a panelled recreation room
a 3-car garage
a complete workshop
cut stone construction
a tower room
a panelled library with book-
    shelves
an interior so clean it glistens
a driveway winding through tall
    trees

a hilltop location
walls 12 to 24 inches thick
hardwood pegged floors
ivy-covered brick exterior
a balcony outside a bedroom
a fireplace in a bedroom
expensive panelling
brick walls with copper trim in
    the kitchen
3-inch thick solid doors with
    massive hinges
hand-carved woodwork
a dark room
a sun deck
a foot bridge

These are but a very few of the literally thousands of features that will, coupled with a good listing, make the house a hot listing—a target house. The full-time, active, hardworking real estate man who will recognize these, and will practice selling people to houses rather than houses to people will be sure of his sale *before* he leaves the office. He will thus have more time to make more sales and his commissions will soon double, then triple!

### Qualifying questions must be used in the proper sequence

The first thing you MUST know at the outset,

1.  Are they buyers?

Many prospects are buyers in mind but not in fact. They have a desire to buy, but not the means. This must be determined immediately, but with tact and finesse. A feeling of trust and confidence would not be generated by the person who bluntly asked, "How much money do you have?" or any other brutally personal question.

How much nicer it sounds to say, "How much do you people want to use as a down payment?" I used this question because it was *not* offensive: it allowed the prospects to maintain the privacy of their financial status, and yet it provided me with the information

I needed. Should the answer be, "How much do we need?" then, depending on the section of the country where you are in business, and the local requirements of the various loaning agencies, you would answer, "Ten (twenty, or thirty) percent of the purchase price" (whatever the case may be).

### They may be ready and willing, but are they able?

There are, of course, V.A., FHA, V.A.-FHA, MGIC (Mortgage Guarantee Insurance Corporation), land contracts, and second mortgages, which all must be discussed if requested by the purchaser. Nevertheless, HERE and NOW it must be determined whether or not you are working with people who actually have on hand sufficient cash for a down payment on a home, as well as a few hundred dollars extra to cover closing cost. In other words, ARE THEY BUYERS? Unless you can completely satisfy yourself on this issue, you are risking a loss of valuable time to go any farther. I suggest you don't.

Assuming they are able to buy, both from cash on hand and monthly income, the next step is to determine,

2. Are they ready to buy?
   Do they have a house to sell before they can buy?
   a. If the answer is yes, they are not BUYERS, they are SELLERS.
   b. If I took the time to show them homes to buy, and they found one they liked, it is almost certain that before we could get their house sold the one they had found would be seen, liked, and purchased by someone else. Then we'd be right back where we started.
   c. The best way to serve these people is to list their home and explain that when it is sold they are then in the position to buy the home of their choice without the risk of losing it while waiting for theirs to sell.
3. Are they motivated to buy?
   Your sale hinges on determining this accurately.
   a. If they are not motivated buyers, they are not buyers.
   b. They *are* motivated if:
      1) They have sold their home and must surrender possession.
      2) They have been transferred into the community and
         a) are living in a motel,

      b) are staying with friends, or

      c) their furniture is in storage or is en route.

3) They are renters and have surrendered their lease, and have a deadline to move.

4) They are newly married and

      a) find it undesirable to live with in-laws,

      b) want a home waiting when they return from their honeymoon, or

      c) have just purchased furniture with an established delivery date.

5) Illness or other circumstances make it absolutely essential that parents or other relatives be taken into their home, and a special residence must be acquired to accomplish this.

c. There are some minor motivations that might be considered, such as a sudden promotion, increase in income, inheritance, desire for income property (duplex, triplex, or apartment house). The advisability of working with these less-motivated buyers is strictly the decision of the individual real estate man.

### You can never sell a house tomorrow

I stayed mainly with the major motivations. I had to know if they were ready, willing and able to buy TODAY, not tomorrow, next week, or next month, but TODAY, because TODAY WAS THE DAY I WAS GOING TO SELL THEM! I learned this by asking them the questions suggested by the information I needed as listed above. Once I had found out IF they could buy, the next step was to learn WHAT they would buy. And the bow-and-arrow technique almost invariably revealed this information by uncovering the necessary clues through a series of probing questions. Then I knew the house they were most likely to buy BEFORE we left the office.

### Probing questions reveal vital clues

To receive fast and repeated success from the bow-and-arrow method, it became necessary for me to train myself to watch for the clues, spoken or implied by my prospects, that would tell me during the qualifying period the house they would buy before we left the office. If sufficient clues were not volunteered while I was asking the *qualifying* questions, then a technique of *probing* for clues became imperative. Just as the kinds of features which create a target house are without limit, so are the exact kinds of questions used to probe for clues. The questions, of course, depend on the features in your target homes.

One of my first experiences in selling with the bow-and-arrow method netted me three sales in one day, totalling $88,500, and generating a commission of $5,320.

**The purest form of a probing question.** The first sale came about when I asked, along with many other questions, "Is there anything you'd like to have in your house that you haven't mentioned because you believed it unlikely that you'd find it?" My prospect's answer was, "Well, yes, I've always wanted a small greenhouse, but I don't imagine there's much chance of that." One of the target homes of my selected 10 percent indeed had a greenhouse, and the sale was made.

**Most any house would do if it had a garden.** The next sale was to a man with a large family. He was a gardener at heart, and he had expressed a desire, in an almost offhand manner, to feed his family with fresh vegetables from their own garden. The clue was there, and I caught it. The house I showed him had five acres with it, two of which I knew had been a vegetable garden for years. He was soon the happy owner.

**They wanted more from a home than just shelter.** The last sale of the day went to a retired couple who dropped the remark that their idea of spending the rest of their lives happily was to catch up on a lifetime of neglected reading, while sitting by a crackling fire. The small home I showed them had the special feature of a library with a large fireplace.

The clues I drew from each of these prospects *suggested* the target homes before we left the office, and my use of many probing questions uncovered them. These questions had to be linked to specific, unique features of my list of target homes available at the particular moment of the attempted sale.

### Use only questions for which you have the answer

You may accumulate a group of target homes entirely different than any I have ever handled; therefore, your probing questions will be governed by the unique features at your disposal at one time or another. There is no standard set of questions to guide you, but I will demonstrate the *type* of questions I used in some specific instances that should clarify the application of this method in a general way.

Again, keep in mind that the homes I had to offer any prospect had already been selected as part of the top 10 percent of the available listings. In other words, there was little likelihood that the prospects would object to the quality and desirability of any of them. It remained, then, only to determine which of these selected homes they were most likely to buy. This would be the target home. Pinpointing the one house which would best suit one particular family was accomplished by uncovering the clue to a particular feature or features that would appeal to their conscious or subconscious desires. When the appeal was strong enough they were motivated to want to purchase the property immediately.

### Double satisfaction eliminates buyer hesitation

In such a case the prospects are not only satisfied with the property in general because it is a top ten percenter, but also they are pleased and delighted with a certain feature far beyond their hopes and expectations. They are motivated to buy at once because they believe there is little hope that they will ever find such a combination again.

We are dealing with the percentage of sales made in relation to the number of prospects as we discuss the bow-and-arrow method. I discovered that the percentage of sales I made increased dramatically when I probed diligently for the clue that would indicate a desire for a home with a unique feature: one that I might have in my list of target homes.

### All they need plus a little of their heart's desire is irresistible

Remember, everyone has within himself, sometimes close to the surface, sometimes buried deep, a strong desire for ONE particular feature that they don't really expect to find when they purchase a home. Find that desire and fill it, and you have a SURE SALE.

First, of course, you will qualify the *logical* needs and desires. If the prospect is a bricklayer by trade, he is an unlikely candidate for a frame house, and you would have a strike against you if you tried to sell a gas company employee an electrically heated home. Conversely, the electrician will be impressed with the electrical circuits, the plumber with elegant bathroom fixtures, copper water pipes, and so forth. This is elementary. The *quick sale* will come from the probing questions. They will reveal that unique feature desired above the standard requirements of the buyer.

For example:

Q. Does your family have any hobbies?

A. Our oldest son rebuilds old cars.

> Target: Home with 3-car garage, giving room for mechanical work, or

A. I like to refinish furniture.

> Target: Home with a complete workshop, or

A. I'm an amateur photographer.

> Target: House complete with darkroom.

Q. What type of furniture do you prefer?

A. We like heavy, solid Victorian furniture.

> Target: Home with cathedral ceilings and exposed beams, or with hand-carved woodwork, or with solid doors with massive hinges, or with a spiral staircase.

Q. Is your family interested in the arts?

A. We have a daughter who's quite a painter.

> Target: A home with one of the following: a screened porch, a sun deck, a tower room, a large bay window, a foot bridge, a bedroom with a balcony or a fireplace, a wooded lot with a small stream, or

A. We're all musically inclined.

> Target: A house with a music room.

Q. Do you entertain much?

A. We have many relatives, and frequent business guests.

> Target: A home with a guest house, a panelled recreation room, three fireplaces, or a 3-car garage.

Q. What part of the country did you grow up in?

A. We both came from the New England states.

> Target: A home with an ivy-covered brick exterior, a hilltop location, cut stone construction, inside-outside thermostatically-controlled heating plant.

A. We're from the South.

Target: A home with a colonnaded entrance, artistically designed flower garden, a driveway through tall trees, a dormitory-type bedroom, a fireplace in the bedroom, or a bedroom with a balcony.

A. We lived in the Midwest.

Target: A home with a slate roof with copper gutters, stained glass windows, a panelled library, or brick walls with copper trim in the kitchen.

A. We're westerners.

Target: A home with a corral and stable, or pegged hardwood floors, a dormitory-type bedroom, or air conditioning.

When it appears that direct questions are becoming a bit tiresome, as they will, the probing should be continued by modifying the questioning into the form of general conversation. I proceeded in this manner: I would discuss current sports, and if the prospect turned out to be a tennis buff, I would give consideration to the target home close to the country club; a baseball fan might want to live near the ball park. When one of my target homes had outstanding plantings and landscaping, I would steer the conversation to gardening, or I would talk about civic affairs and church affiliations, with the thought for a need for meeting space, such as recreation rooms, screened porches, large lots, or guest houses.

### Like keys, it's always the last question that opens the door

I might then speak of our local library, and about books, and a house with a library: quiet rooms with stained-glass windows, hideaway rooms, and a tower room. If books didn't seem to interest them, I'd then shift to architecture, and the romance of large brick houses on hilltops, plantation homes with colonnaded entrances, Victorian homes with slate roofs, spiral staircases, panelling and ornate woodwork. I would see how they responded to conversation about country living, horseback riding, nearby fishing lakes, wooded lots. I'd discuss a little of science and astronomy—maybe they had a hidden desire to own a telescope some day, and would therefore be interested in a sun deck or a tower room or a hilltop location.

In short, I would continue to go from topic to topic, leading the conversation but being sure to let the prospects participate; searching and probing until sooner or later, as sure as the sunrise, they would drop a clue that was the tipoff to which of my target homes they were most likely to buy. It worked for me time and time and time again. Why shouldn't it work for you? TRY IT!

### The elusive prospect

Some prospects would answer my questions either untruthfully or incompletely, even though I was trying hard to find the best possible home for them. Others could not be drawn into conversation, but just answered my questions with one or two words. I had to discover another way to find out the things I wanted to know.

### If the answer is too emphatic, chances are it's untrue

When I sensed I had a prospect who was giving me false or incomplete answers, I resorted to the 'courtroom' technique: that is, the lawyer's trick of asking the same question two different ways, and talking about something else in between the questions. If the first answer was stated emphatically, then almost invariably the prospect meant the opposite. There is a way of testing this.

"You have indicated that you want a 3-bedroom brick home with a basement, garage and fireplace, in a top location. It will save us a lot of time if you will tell me approximately what you expect to spend."

"Twenty thousand dollars is our top. We *will not* go above that."

As a real estate man who is acquainted with the market, you know that if he really means a $20,000 top price then he must compromise on the features of the property he has asked for, because you know that no such property exists for $20,000.

**Setting him up for the test question.** The proper procedure now is to change the subject completely. It is imperative to take his mind away from the cost of houses and the amount of money he wants to spend. Then, when the dollar question is asked again in a different form, his declaration of a maximum expenditure will not be so fresh in his mind that he feels the need to defend or accentuate it—if, in fact, he *did not* mean the $20,000 limit.

For the next ten minutes or so I talked to him about his family, and how important it is for the children to be raised in a good neighborhood. Then I discussed his work, and the friends and business associates whom he will probably be entertaining in his new home. I specifically pointed out that serious consideration should be given, on the day he buys it, to the time in the future when he may sell his house; i.e., its resale value. As a final statement before rephrasing my key question, I invariably tossed in the thought-provoking observation that frequently the cheaper house turns out to be the most expensive. If it is not in good condition and does not fit the buyers' needs, it will have to be renovated or remodelled.

**A capsule education in home ownership.** Then I was ready to determine if a dollar barrier really existed. It might be well to note, as was covered more thoroughly in an earlier chapter, that quite frequently the feature that a prospect is positive in saying he will not buy is the very feature he *will* buy. That in itself is a clue to be watched for and tested for validity by the alert real estate man.

**The test of desire over dollars.** Ten minutes and a dozen questions later, I'd say: "I have a special home I would like very much to show to you. It has everything you've asked for, plus a wooded lot, a huge kitchen, and refrigerated cooling. It's $32,000, and it's an outstanding buy! In fact, it's so outstanding I'd really like you to see it."

Hesitation—then, "Okay, let's look at it."

He has tipped his hand. He DIDN'T mean the $20,000 limit!

This same technique of question-diversion-rephrased question will work on location, type of architecture, or any other specific item that the prospect appears to be against, too emphatically.

### The mystery of human behavior

Is there a real estate man anywhere who has not had prospects tell him they absolutely would not consider anything other than a new, one-story house close in, only to have those same prospects, a few days later, buy an old, two-story home, five miles out, from a competitor?

### The uncommunicative prospect

If there's anything more disconcerting to the real estate man than the prospect who talks too much it's the one who won't talk at all.

Attempting to apply the bow-and-arrow method to the silent prospect is a frustrating experience. To uncover the clues, I *had* to get them to talk.

When I was first faced with this dilemma, knowing that I had willing buyers because they qualified as such, I discovered a secret: every man has *one* favorite topic that he will discuss with fervor, if not passion, merely on hearing it mentioned. Consequently, to discover what that topic was I frequently carried on a conversation with myself, going from subject to subject, waiting for my prospect to plunge in. From skiing to stamp collecting, baseball to boats, foundries to featherstitching—literally from A to Z, I poked and probed, teased and tempted every subject I could think of until suddenly I hit the right one. Then I was drowned in a torrent of conversation which eventually produced the clue that revealed the inner man and the thing he longed for; the feature that would most appeal to him.

It was a mental exercise that improved with usage. As time went by I picked up little gems of information in my casual reading and stored them away to be brought out later and bounced off the sounding board of my silent prospects.

### How to sell like you've never sold before

There is *always* a clue: find it and your sale is made. The bow-and-arrow method will do that for you. It is one of the Golden Keys to faster, surer sales.

It must now be obvious that for a real estate man to operate successfully on a high income level, it is an absolute necessity for him to develop and practice IMAGINATION, INGENUITY, CONCENTRATION, and ATTENTIVENESS to the extremely complex minds and personalities of his buyers. But this much I assure you: if you will perfect and use the technique of bow-and-arrow selling, YOU WILL SELL LIKE YOU'VE NEVER SOLD BEFORE!!

### Points to remember

1. The time needed to make each sale MUST be reduced in order to earn $30,000 or more per year.
2. Shotgun-selling, i.e., showing innumerable houses to each prospect, is amateurish and a dreadful waste of precious hours.

3. Remember Jim, who had a 99 to 1 shot in his favor—and he *lost*.

4. The secret in qualifying is; first determine *if* they can buy, then *what* they will buy, BEFORE you leave the office!

5. Probing questions will uncover the clue to the house your prospects WANT to buy.

## CHAPTER 12

# FIFTEEN MINUTES' OVERTIME
# GAVE ME THREE SALES
# IN ONE DAY

To earn TWENTY-FOUR HUNDRED DOLLARS in one day is a rare experience in any man's life. The chance for me to accomplish this presented itself one night because I was not in a hurry to leave the office. I had remained fifteen minutes past closing time when opportunity walked in the door in the form of an out-of-state buyer desperately looking for a four-bedroom home.

It was the opening scene of a three-act play—three sales linked together which were to earn me $2,400. Working overtime simply gave me the occasion—the three sales resulted from techniques, properly applied in each case.

This is what had to be done:

1. Find the hard-to-find property.
2. Convince the owner to sell.
3. Locate a home for the first seller to buy.
4. Locate a home for the second seller to buy.
5. Correlate closings and possession dates compatible with all parties.

### The second sale is the link that forms the chain

This experience proved to be an ideal example of a CHAIN of sales, and is an excellent way to add additional sales to your year's total. It should be pointed out, however, that if a link is missing, there can be no chain. That is to say, when a series of three or four sales can be linked together, if the second sale is not made, numbers three and four will never come about. From this viewpoint, making that second sale in the chain becomes tremendously important. If you fail to make the second sale in the series, not one sale is lost, but all those that would follow as well. Our object is always to make more sales, not fewer. Therefore, let's dwell a moment on why the number two sale is frequently lost, and how to prevent that.

### Don't close your mind when you close the sale

The second sale in the chain is often lost because real estate people can't seem to remember the simple fact that when a SELLER's home is sold, he becomes a BUYER. It is positively incredible to me to think of the number of salesmen who present a purchase agreement to an owner, obtain his signature, thank him, and walk out of the house without another word. When they do this, they often turn their backs on an easy SECOND sale and very possibly on a CHAIN OF SALES. Let that not ever happen to you! ALWAYS ask the owners of the home you've just sold if they intend to buy another home—it may start a chain of sales. You might even earn TWENTY-FOUR HUNDRED DOLLARS IN ONE DAY!

### The best possible type of prospect

People who purchase a home immediately after selling are buying at a time when they are best prepared to buy. Their thinking is clear and their enthusiasm is high, and their minds haven't been influenced by advice from friends and relatives on what to buy or not to buy. Their perspective is not warped by having their attention submitted to all shapes and sizes of properties during endless days of house hunting, by a variety of real estate people.

The real estate man who is wise enough to engineer an *immediate* sale to people who have suddenly become buyers by virtue of their house being sold will find it to be one of the easiest sales of his year. Remember, with each day that passes the task of finding them a satisfactory home will become increasingly more difficult. If too many days go by you will very likely lose them. If their purpose for selling is to buy a home more suitable to their needs or desires, there is no acceptable excuse why you shouldn't sell them their next home within 24 hours. Get with them quickly, work hard, and close fast!

I have had many experiences with series of linked sales—as few as two and as many as five, and generally they were spread over a period of many days. The example I have chosen to demonstrate how this works is the one, however, that produced the largest commission within the shortest time, and brought me closer to my million dollars worth of sales in one year.

## THE ONLY LIGHTED OFFICE ON REAL ESTATE ROW LURED AN OUT-OF-STATE BUYER

I was alone in the office. The wall clock read 9:15 and I was about to switch off the lights when a car pulled up in front. A man came through the door asking if we were still open, and when I had invited him in, he said,

"I was heading for my motel when I saw your office lights. I need a four-bedroom home and I'm not having much luck. Can you help me?"

After some deliberation, I replied, "I don't know of a single four-bedroom home on the market, but if such a property is available I'll find it for you. Describe what you want and tell me your price range."

I had made an instant friend. No other real estate person had made him such an offer. There were very few four-bedroom homes in our area, and even fewer for sale. He knew this and was grateful for my sincere offer to help.

In the subsequent qualifying period, I learned that he was an executive of a national concern. With six children, he needed four bedrooms. His company had transferred him to our community, and was paying his expenses during the necessary time for house hunting. That time was rapidly running out and both he and the company were anxious that his housing problem be settled. I sent him off to his motel with the assurance that his problem was now mine, and advised him to relax and let me struggle with it.

### The search

Early the next morning I sat at my desk concentrating on how to fulfill my promise of the night before. The answer was obvious. I would find a four-bedroom home for this man by going out and searching for it.

I cruised street after street, scoured neighborhood after neighborhood, and then all at once I turned a corner and there it was—a large, two-story brick home with classic lines and an impressive appearance. The house unquestionably contained four or more bedrooms. It could be the answer to my problem.

Step One was completed. I had found the HARD-TO-FIND. It was now a matter of convincing the owners to let me sell it.

### A foot in the door in the form of a compliment

An elderly gentleman answered my knock. I told him my name and business, and asked if by chance he was interested in selling his home. His answer was a pleasant but firm no, and it seemed that I was defeated before I could get started. To forestall his closing the door, I quickly said,

"The reason I stopped by is that your home is very attractive, and I felt sure it had four bedrooms. Does it?"

When he said it had, I explained that I had a client who needed a house with four bedrooms. Then I glanced over his shoulder to the living room beyond.

"It looks like an exceptionally lovely home. I'd enjoy seeing it."

He hesitated a moment and then, like any proud homeowner, he stepped aside and invited me to come in and look around.

I had accomplished the first half of Step Two.

### A surprising revelation

It was indeed a lovely home; large, bright, and immaculately clean. It was made to order for my prospect of the night before, Mr. Merrill. The man introduced himself as Mr. Black, and we were soon joined by his wife. I complimented them on their beautiful home, and the couple beamed with pride.

"There's one thing I don't quite understand. If just the two of you live here, why do you feel you need such a huge home, with all of the expenses and work involved?"

Mr. Black answered, "We raised our family in this house, and Mrs. Black feels so much of our lives have been spent here she doesn't want to give it up."

Mrs. Black came back with the surprising retort, "Oh, that's not quite the case; I wouldn't mind a smaller home at all. But Dad has his garden and the workshop he enjoys so much. He even planted the trees around the place when we first moved here. I don't think. . . ."

"Now, wait a minute," interrupted her husband. "I've thought for a long time that we should get a smaller place, but I never believed you would agree to it."

So, suddenly, it was out in the open. Each one thought the other was so attached to the home that moving was out of the question! I felt that I was in business. My next job was to convince the Blacks it was to their advantage to let me sell their home.

### A flawless plan that was nearly impossible to refuse

I first explained very carefully that I had a client whom I was fairly positive would buy their home. We discussed the market value at some length, and finally agreed on a $33,000 price. Then I asked if I could call Mr. Merrill and have him come right over, but the request seemed to frighten them.

"This is moving too fast—we'll have to think it over," was Mr. Black's reply.

"Mr. Merrill is going to buy the first good, four-bedroom home he comes across. I don't think we should lose him."

"But we must have somewhere to go. We can't move in with the neighbors," Mrs. Black protested.

"Leave that up to me," I said. "Let me make a suggestion and see what you think of it. I'll call Mr. Merrill and have him come over. If he's willing to buy your house, I'll have him sign a sales agreement and put up a deposit. Then I'll place a contingency clause in the agreement stating that at any time on or before ten days you may withdraw your property from the market and the contract will be null and void. I guarantee that in less than ten days I will find a smaller home for you, and for less money than you will receive for this one. In fact, I have a home in mind this very moment that I would like you to see."

Mr. Black thought a moment. "Under those terms, go ahead."

I had now completed Step Two, convincing the owner to sell.

I dialed Mr. Merrill's office and told him a little of what had happened. He said he would leave at once. From the look on his face when I met him at the front door, I knew the first sale was made. The next order of business was to take him to my office and draw the sales agreement. I told the Blacks I would be back in less than an hour to show them the home I had mentioned earlier.

### With their house sold, they were free to make a decision

I soon returned to pick up the Blacks. The house I had in mind for them was a small, charming custom-built ranch house with a workshop in the basement for Mr. Black, a large, beautiful kitchen for Mrs. Black, and a flower and vegetable garden out in the back for them both.

I had no selling to do. When we had completed a thorough inspection of the property, I asked Mr. Black if he were ready to buy the house. He answered yes without hesitation. (This would not have been possible if I had not arranged for them to sign a sales agreement on their present home first.) As we waited at the office for the sales agreement to be typed, the Blacks signed a statement removing the no longer needed contingency from the Merrill contract.

Step Three was fulfilled.

### Forging the third link in the chain

I still had to get the signatures of the owners of the home the Blacks bought. Thirty minutes later I made that stop and obtained the signatures of the Finns without delay. Mr. Finn then surprised me by saying,

"Now *we* need a house."

He proceeded to tell me that he and his wife had come from a farming community, and for some time had had their hearts set on buying an old farm-style house with five or ten acres so that they could raise their children in the country. I had such a property in my TOP 10 PERCENT. I described it to him in detail. Mr. Finn was interested, so I called the owners for permission to see the farm.

As we pulled up to the large white house, the sunset shone through one of the many willow trees that bordered the back of the property. The grounds were a mass of flowers, and on one side was a vegetable garden an acre or more in size.

### A perfect matching of house to buyer

From the silence that settled over my buyers, I felt that very little selling would be needed with this property. I was right. I knew it was not necessary to ask the Finns if they wanted to buy the home. I drove to the office, typed the contract, and they signed it.

Step Four was accomplished, and my chain was complete.

After I took the Finns home, I reflected on the events of the day: three sales, totalling $81,000, with earned commissions of $4,860. And all because I had stayed fifteen minutes past closing time the night before.

### A comprehensive review of this chain of sales

1. The whole thing started by working a little past closing time.
2. I made the prospect welcome even though the hour was late.
3. A sincere promise to help bonded the prospect.
4. Thorough qualification proved him to be a buyer.
5. My search for the hard-to-find house was diligent and determined.
6. Entrance to the house, so necessary to get the listing, was accomplished with old-fashioned flattery.
7. Selling the seller on the idea of permitting me to sell his home was a matter of qualifying the seller.
    a. There were visual clues that a sale was possible. Two persons were living in an eight-room, two-story house. There were stairs to climb, which is often difficult for elderly people, large grounds requiring care beyond their ability, and an investment representing locked-in dollars that could be released by exchanging this large home for a smaller, less expensive house.
    b. Probing questions uncovered the startling fact that each

was willing to sell but mistakenly believed that the other was not.

c. The convincer was the fact that it could all be accomplished quickly, because I already had a buyer for their house, as well as a house which I felt was made to order for them.

d. Remembering that sellers are not buyers until their property is sold, I had to convince them they should first make a deal to sell their house BEFORE they looked at the house they were to buy.

e. The contingency clause was their safeguard, as it gave them the right to withdraw if they should not like the house I was to show them, and it opened the way for me to proceed.

8. Proof that buyers are most easily handled immediately after the sale of their property is evidenced by the fact that they readily purchased *the one and only house I showed them.*

9. When the possibility of the third sale in the chain became evident, it was easily consummated, not by accident or a stroke of luck, but because I handled special houses in the top 10 percent, and because I sold people to houses instead of houses to people. I had the right property ready and waiting when the second sellers became buyers.

Producing a chain of sales is much like producing a play, except that you write the script, speak the lines, and manipulate the actors as you go along.

### Points to remember

1. If everyone else in the office goes home, you have a monopoly.
2. A little overtime can result in a lot of business.
3. If you can't give them a house, give them a promise.
4. Don't be too proud to ring a doorbell.
5. There's a house for every buyer: if you don't have it—go get it!

# CHAPTER 13

# HOW I SOLD "I WANT TO THINK IT OVER" PROSPECTS BY CREATING A CRISIS

---

The fifty or more sales that it takes to make up a MILLION DOLLAR YEAR will be reduced by at least 20 percent if the real estate man gives in to the prospect who says,

"I want to think it over."

In my early years I heard that statement many times. It was a delaying tactic that killed sale after sale. If I was to become a top producer I had to do something about counteracting its use.

I used an excellent technique which is best described as "creating a crisis." Executed properly, it puts the prospect in the position where he MUST MAKE A DECISION. It tosses the "I want to think it over" tactic right out the window.

### The fear of losing the home must be greater than the fear of buying it

I discovered what caused some persons to postpone their decision. What they really meant, instead of wanting to think it over, was that they were frightened and lacked the courage to buy the house at this moment. I learned to fight fire with fire: I would take the house away from them, and thus create a fear of losing it which was greater than their fear of agreeing to buy it!

You can never make a sale *tomorrow;* you can only make it *today.* Creating a crisis was designed to do just that. Perfecting a sophisticated technique like this one is the mark of a professional and its use is absolutely mandatory to earn TWENTY-FIVE THOU-SAND DOLLARS OR MORE a year in the real estate business. This technique, like all the others, MUST be practiced, rehearsed, pol-ished and refined. Once you have mastered it you will have a magic, money-making method, unmatched for closing a sale. Let's take a look at how it's done.

## CREATING A CRISIS

When I have found a home for prospects that fills their needs and desires, falls within their ability to pay, and that they want to own but lack the courage to buy, I believe that I am professionally obligated to apply whatever measures are necessary to guide them through their fears and worries to the point where they are willing to make the purchase.

If I fail them, and permit them to indulge in a period of "think-ing it over," something will very likely occur to deter their pur-chase. They will talk to friends, receive advice from relatives, or look at more houses, and all the while their pointless fears will be magnified out of reason. From this point on, they are looking at second-choice houses, and their perspective will become blurred. Finally, out of desperation or exhaustion, or both, they will buy a home that doesn't fit their needs and desires nearly as well as the house I *should* have sold them the first day they saw it. By allowing this to happen, I have failed my obligation to them. To fulfill this obligation, I use the method of creating a crisis.

### Lack of communication equals fear as a sales-stopper

It must be made clear that the "creating a crisis" technique can be applied only to those prospects who have moved through all the steps of the sale, willingly and affirmatively, to the moment of signing the sales agreement. Then, at that point, they come to a standstill. It seems that no amount of persuasion or encouragement can get them past the final but all-important act of signing their names. Sometimes it's fear, and sometimes it's a lack of communication. Which it is, you must determine. Usually, those being deterred by fear resort to the "we want to think it over" defense, and those who are stymied by a lack of communication simply sit, say nothing, and refuse to respond in any manner.

### Conquering "buyer's jitters"

In the first instance, since the prospects do need and want the house, it logically follows that they will sign an agreement to buy if the fear is removed. *In this case our unusual technique is a matter of cancelling out one fear with another.* At this stage their thinking is a composite of many negatives: they're acting too hastily; maybe there's a house somewhere they'll like better; they are paying too much for it; maybe they should have had some of their friends look at the house; maybe somewhere, somehow, they have overlooked something; it's a big step—they should sleep on it.

### Taking the home away from them regenerates the strength of desire

WE MUST REVERSE this kind of thinking. The quickest and surest way to wipe out all of these thoughts is to take the house away from them. With the house gone, their fears are gone. We're all back where we started.

Here is how the property is taken away from them. Agree with them that maybe they should take some time to think it over, BUT. . . .

Then we direct and control their thinking toward the property now that they are NOT buying the house. It is pointed out that, just as THEY liked the house, OTHER people will like it. The property will continue to be shown while they're "thinking it over." They are told that it is positively uncanny how, when one party becomes interested in a home, there are suddenly one or two others anxious to buy it. These statements are all true, and are calculated to "take the house away from them."

### While they are thinking it over they probably will lose it

The clincher that I always use is a point-blank statement: "I sincerely believe that the chances are very high this house will be gone when you return from 'thinking it over.' " In other words, they will lose it; it will be taken away from them.

The prospects' minds are no longer occupied with fears—now they are confronted with making the decision: should they buy this house which they really want, or should they take the chance of losing it? They have a choice. They realize there is really no genuine purpose in thinking it over, no sensible reason to take the chance of losing the home they want. Their decision is almost always to buy.

### The buyers must be forced to reveal
### the obstacle delaying them

When the problem is a lack of communication between you and the buyer, or between the buyer and his wife, you must resort to the tried-and-true technique of probing questions. To list all of the things that could block a sale would fill another book, but, as an example, your probing questions might reveal which one is the decision-maker of the family. Often it's the quiet, reserved one.

Frequently the buyers are embarrassed to ask a particular question, such as the interest rate on their loan, or whether the price could be lowered a little, whether the sellers would leave the garden tools, and so forth. Such matters are very small problems for you, but sales-stoppers from their point of view. In short, if you know they WANT to buy but they won't tell you why they're hesitating, you simply must search and probe with questions and conversation until you discover what the obstacle is so that you may remove it. Once that is done you have your sale.

### How fear is overcome by taking
### the house away from them

Mr. and Mrs. Moore were an average couple with two children. He was employed as a foreman in an electronics plant. They had sold their home in the city and were looking forward to living in the suburbs where there were large lawns, tree-lined streets, and clean fresh air. They didn't have to surrender possession of the home they sold for sixty days, and so felt that they had worlds of time for house hunting.

They came into my office on their first day of looking. I qualified them, and they were buyers in anyone's book. From clues I picked up during our conversation, I believed I had two or three homes any one of which would suit them well. Which one they chose would be a simple matter of personal taste.

### The decision, "This is it," can be read
### in the faces of the buyers

It was early evening when they arrived, and after dark when we returned from a close inspection of three properties. All the other sales people had gone home, and I had the office to myself. I had observed the Moores closely as we toured the homes, watching for facial expressions, a glance between husband and wife, or any one of the many tip-off clues buyers give when they're in a house they would like to own. I knew which one they had liked the best.

### Your professional opinion adds to the buyers'
### conviction that it is the right house

"The house on Elm Street is the house you're looking for."
The wife answered, "Yes, I like that home very much."
Her husband agreed, "I do too. It's a nice place."
Then we discussed the distance to the train, shopping centers and schools. We talked about the school system, life as it's lived in the suburbs, and the recreational facilities. Everything was progressing very nicely. We moved a step closer to the sale when Mr. Moore asked what financing was available, the interest rate, and the loan charges. When those items had been thoroughly covered, I thought the time had come to ask,
"Shall I draw up the agreement?"
And then came those dreaded words, "We like the house, but we want to think it over."

### A request to think it over
### is an admission of cold feet

As pleasantly as I could, but as firmly as I dared, I said,
"Mr. Moore, what is there to think over? You have said that you like the house very much. You agreed that it's priced right. The location is excellent, the financing is good, all that's left to do now is for you to buy it. Tell me, Mr. Moore, what is there to talk over that we can't do right here and now?"

This is the point at which most buyers begin to experience cold feet. They begin to be afraid they're going to do something wrong. Mr. and Mrs. Moore were no exception.

Mrs. Moore spoke up. "This is the first day we've looked. We just can't buy a house the first day out."

"Why not?" I asked. "As any good real estate man would, I showed you the best houses I had, first. And, secondly, I have done your househunting for you long before you ever came in the office. I did it when I listed the fine homes. In my opinion, you have seen the three best homes in your category, and you have chosen one of them as your preference. I can think of no logical reason why you shouldn't buy it. If there is one, let's discuss it."

I waited for a response, and, with none forthcoming, I concluded my comments: "The proper moment to buy is when you have found the right house. You have found it. Let me draw up the agreement."

There was another short period of silence. Then Mr. Moore said, "Mr. Gardiner, no doubt all you say is true, but we're going to think it over tonight and we'll see you tomorrow." And they stood up to leave.

The battle was lost, but not the war. To save the day I needed a crisis.

### Planting the seed of fear of losing the house

I assumed an entirely new attitude. I became friendly and casual, as if our recent serious conversation had never taken place.

"Fine," I said, "but let me call you after I've set up some appointments to see a few more homes. Now that we have given up on the Elm Street house, I'll really have to do some digging to find houses anywhere near equal to it. I'll try to call you by ten or ten-thirty."

"Oh, we haven't given up on the Elm Street house," Mrs. Moore said quickly.

"I think we should forget about the Elm Street property," I said, slowly ushering them to the door, "I'll have something nice for you to look at and, who knows, maybe it will be something you'll like as well."

"But why should we forget about it?" pursued Mrs. Moore, a little anxiously.

To be convincing, I had to make a little display of dramatics. I paused significantly: then, in a low and confidential tone of voice, almost as if I were telling a secret, I said,

"I feel very strongly that the Elm Street property will be gone before you get back tomorrow. It is one of our best listings. Other salesmen have been showing it, and other people like it, just as you do. During the years I've been in this business I've come to appreciate how uncanny it is that when there's one buyer for a property, suddenly there are two or three. I can almost sense when a house is about to be sold.

### Inducing your buyers to face up to a decision

"I very respectfully tell you that I believe you are making a mistake by not buying the house tonight, but that is your decision. I don't want to see you disappointed and unhappy tomorrow, so I suggest we forget the Elm Street house, and I'll do my level best to find you a home that I hope you'll like as well."

I had taken it away from them: I had created a crisis. They were now face to face with an unavoidable decision.

### They need only to believe there is a "reasonable" chance of losing the home

The success of my endeavors rested solely on how convincing I had been when I told them if they didn't want to lose the house, they should buy it that night. It wasn't necessary that they be *absolutely sure* they would lose the house: I needed only to have them believe that there was a *reasonable chance* this would happen. If they really wanted to own the home, they would not be willing to take that chance. Incidentally, I have seen many, many people wait overnight to decide on a house only to lose it to another buyer. It happens disturbingly often.

### Encapsulated logic clears the path to closing a sale

Mr. and Mrs. Moore stood silently preoccupied, and I left them with their thoughts. Finally I said,

"If there's some doubt in your minds about the quality of the home, the price, or any other matter that we can't clear up right here and now, then probably you would be wise to pass it up for the time being. However, if you are as pleased and satisfied with the house as I think you are, then it's just a matter of making the decision.

"Now, whether you make that decision tonight or tomorrow doesn't change a thing: the decision still has to be made. I believe the time to make that decision is right now. It takes a little courage, and a little confidence, but it can be the difference between owning the home you want, or losing it."

Mr. Moore thought for a few moments, then turned to his wife and said, "What do you think?"

She answered, "Let's buy it."

Mr. Moore smiled at me and said, "You've sold us. Draw up the papers."

**You serve your buyers well
when you force a decision**

In the months and years to come, I had coffee with the Moores in their home many times, and I never knew prouder homeowners. We often laughed about the night that they almost got out the door. Like many buyers they needed a little urging to make the decision, but taking the property away from them by creating a crisis did the job. My effort was well spent. It earned me SIX HUNDRED FIFTY DOLLARS and added another sale to my million dollar year.

## OPTIONAL USE OF THE THIRD PERSON ENDORSEMENT TECHNIQUE

Creating a crisis is a versatile tool. It may be broadly applied and widely adapted to almost all buyers in their time of indecision. One variation, the THIRD PERSON ENDORSEMENT, can be illustrated by relating the Thornton sale.

Up to a point, the sale had been the same as dozens of others before it. The scenery, the dialogue, and the characters followed the usual pattern.

**You are on top of the situation
if you KNOW which house your buyers like most**

I had just returned to the office from taking a listing on a particularly pretty little home on which the owner had given me a weekend exclusive, when the Thorntons walked into the office. They were a nice couple in their early thirties who were sincerely interested in purchasing a home. (The other side of the story of the weekend exclusive is told in Chapter 20.) After our qualifying session I felt sure my new exclusive was just the house for the Thorntons. Depending on my opinion of the temperament of my buyers, formulated during qualifying, I sometimes showed my best house first, and sometimes last. In the Thornton's case I chose to show them two other homes first for contrast. Whether or not such strategy was necessary I can't be sure, but I do know the Thorntons fell head over heels in love with the last house, as I had expected. They were so excited about it on the trip back to the office that I thought getting them to sign a purchase agreement would be duck soup.

**A quick change of attitude foreshadows
problems to come**

But when I seated them at my desk, it was obvious that a change had taken place. They were like two different people. The wife became sober, withdrawn, and very, very quiet. Mr. Thornton also assumed a very serious attitude, totally opposite from his manner of a few minutes before. He was a little frightened, to be sure, but that was to be expected. However, I was confident that if the situation were handled with a little professional skill I would soon have their signatures on the dotted line.

Mr. Thornton asked endless questions. He seemed to be struggling to enact the role of a wise and prudent buyer. A number of times I attempted to close, but each time Mr. Thornton parried my attempt with a new question. He wanted to know if I thought the taxes would increase; how much time there was left on the furnace warranty; if the roof was a good one; how soon he would have to repaint the house; if there were future assessments to be expected; the best rate of interest on his mortgage that I could guarantee him; how much the fire insurance was and what it covered. On and on the questions came.

### Silent patience is a formidable method of selling

I decided that he felt that as long as he could ask questions he could postpone the terrible moment of the decision to put his name on a document which he didn't understand or completely trust. All this time, Mrs. Thornton sat quietly, listening carefully but not participating in the conversation.

Once I understood what was happening, I relaxed and settled back, fascinated by the drama of this isolated little scene. Finally, Mr. Thornton exhausted his supply of questions. Think as he would, he simply couldn't produce another question that he hadn't asked. The so-called moment of truth in our little encounter was at hand.

### The truth and tenderness technique

Many months before, I had adoped a method I called the "truth and tenderness" technique, to be used at special times. This was one of those times. Mr. Thornton had had his hour on the stage—now it was my turn.

I administered the tenderness by relieving the pressure. I took him off the hot spot he was standing on by suddenly saying, "By the way, Mr. Thornton, are you a baseball fan?" When he said he was, we were off on a short discussion of sports. This led to other topics, and we just sat and visited for a while.

Slowly, and from a distance, I began to guide the conversation back to the subject at hand. I mentioned a young couple to whom I had sold a home, who reminded me of the Thorntons. I described how pleased and happy they were in their new residence. This implied third-person endorsement opened the way for me to convey, indirectly, the truths that I wanted the Thorntons to hear, without the feeling of being pressured. I pointed out the economic wisdom of owning a home, the enforced savings factor, the long-range security, the elevation of credit rating, the tax advantages, the pride of ownership, a man's obligation to his family to furnish them with a home of their own, and the higher degree of respect in the community one has as a homeowner. I covered the subject of buying a home truthfully, tenderly, and overwhelmingly. In fact, I felt I was in rare form and that my listeners would not only be willing but anxious not to let another minute go by without owning a home.

I had hand-drafted a sales contract, and now I said to Mr. Thornton,

"I'll have the secretary type this up so we can see how it looks."

### Procrastination without apparent reason

When he made no immediate objection, I put the girl on it at once. While we waited, I visited once more with Mr. Thornton, trying to determine what made him tick. I knew they were in love with the house, and his down payment was more than adequate, as was his income. Why was he procrastinating? What was causing him to delay doing something he wanted to do very much?

When the girl finished typing the sales agreement, I knew that Mr. Thornton was not yet ready to sign it. I also knew that the take-it-away-from-them type of creating a crisis was not apropos in this instance, for they had said nothing about thinking it over; they just wouldn't sign their names. A different crisis was needed. Just what kind, I wouldn't know until I knew more about Mr. Thornton. I could only learn what I needed to know by probing questions. With luck I would hit it in the first two or three, but it might take ten times that many. So I started to probe.

### Relentless probing becomes mandatory

"What kind of work do you do, Mr. Thornton?" "What city were you originally from?" "What kind of business was your father in?" Each question developed a little conversation. "Where do you usually go on vacation?" "Do you do much bowling?" And on and on. By this time, the neatly typed sales agreement and copies were lying on the desk in front of me. Now *I* was beginning to run out of questions, and I was apparently no nearer the key to this problem than when I started.

I decided to try a different tack. I picked up the sales agreement, offered the original to the husband and a copy to his wife.

"Look this over," I said, "and if there's anything you don't understand, I'll try to explain it." I sat back and waited.

Mr. Thornton read his copy over rather hurriedly. He seemed to be anxious to let go of it. Without comment, he laid it back on my desk. Mrs. Thornton was studying her copy very carefully. She was engrossed in all the details and it was some time before she finished. Then she, too, laid her copy on my desk.

"Does everything seem to be in order?" I asked.

They both nodded.

Now where do I go? I thought to myself. Deciding to stay on the positive approach, I said to Mr. Thornton, "By the way, who do you intend to have do your moving?"

"Oh," he said, "Mrs. Thornton makes all the decisions of that nature." And he laughed.

There was my answer. For over two hours I had been talking to the WRONG PERSON. I knew in just a moment or two I would create a crisis which would make or break my sale, but first I had a little preparation to do.

### The buyer had to be forced to refuse to sign

I turned the sales agreement with the bottom toward Mr. Thornton, and laid my pen down just above the line to sign. Then I said,

"Mr. Thornton, the first step necessary to own that home you want so much is to put your signature on this agreement."

His response was a very unconvincing, "I think my wife and I had better talk this over. After all, it's the biggest purchase we'll ever make, and we shouldn't rush into it." (HE thought he and his wife should talk it over, but no one had asked HER and SHE was the decision-maker!)

### If they were going to buy, the wife had to make the first move

Now was the time. I sat silently looking at Mr. Thornton, as if meditating and analyzing what he had said. Then I turned to his wife.

"Mrs. Thornton, I'm sure you know what a fine man you have for a husband. He wants to buy this house for you. I believe he wants to give you as many of the fine things in life as he can. All he asks from you is your moral support, your confidence, and the assurance that you are with him. I think he deserves that much, don't you?"

She looked at me a little wide-eyed for a few long moments; then, with great deliberation, she picked up the pen and signed her name on the bottom line. It was one of the few times I ever saw the wife sign first.

**She was afforded the opportunity to make the decision under the guise of a demonstration of confidence**

Again I had created a crisis. There was some danger involved, as there is in all crises, because, had she become offended with my frank outburst, or had her husband resented it, my sale would have gone up in smoke. Fortunately neither of those things happened. Mr. Thornton readily added his signature, and once they were outside the fearsome tension of my office, they quickly reverted to the happy, chattering, delightful people that they had been earlier in the day. The only difference was that they were now homeowners.

**Points to remember**

1. "We want to think it over," usually means, "We haven't the courage to buy."
2. The degree of the buyers' desire must be made greater than their fears.
3. If they want a house and don't buy it, somewhere YOU failed.
4. When you have lost control, create a crisis.
5. Determine who is the decision-maker in the family.
6. Have the courage to claim your sale and FORCE your claim.

# CHAPTER 14

# HOW I CONVINCE A SELLER TO ACCEPT A FAIR OFFER

---

How many real estate men have been blasted with the words *"We're Not Going To Give This House Away!"* when presenting an offer to a seller? It has happened countless times and will continue to happen as long as there is a real estate profession.

When this happens to you, you should be encouraged rather than discouraged because it is a typical reaction, and techniques have been devised that are nearly infallible in handling such a situation.

### A spoken refusal puts you in control

You can't start selling until someone says "No." Whether it be a reaction such as the one stated above, or one less vehement, you might as well relax and settle back in your chair—you have a long, tough job ahead of you.

Your responsibility is fourfold: to your buyers, to your office, to yourself, AND to your sellers. When the seller says, "No," from that moment on YOU are in control. If he were indecisive, wishy-washy, or wanted to think it over, you would not be in control. Of course, many sellers accept an offer with very little resistance. We are concerned in this chapter with how to handle a seller who firmly refuses an offer.

### The ultimate points of conviction

Everything must have a point of beginning, and in this case it is the fact that you have a good and fair offer; otherwise you shouldn't be there. With that in mind, we will study how to bring the seller from his adamant stand of rejection through rational consideration to ultimate acceptance of the offer. We will show him that by refusing a fair offer, he has bought his own house back for the amount of the offer, and thereby has become a real estate speculator. It will be a while before we arrive at this juncture, however. First there are other bridges to cross.

## IN REAL ESTATE THERE ARE TWO PARTIES TO SELL INSTEAD OF ONE

When I came to realize that I had to sell both the buyer and the seller to make a deal, I made a diligent study in preparation for selling the seller. This took me back to when the house was listed. The battle of the price should be fought the day the listing is taken. Experience soon taught me that the time required to convince sellers to price their house properly was the most important time spent during the entire sale. As I see it I was, in fact, making my sale then and there. Furthermore, if I could not convince the seller to list his house at what was, in my opinion, a fair market price, the wisest thing I could do was to refuse the listing. I have refused many. By doing so I could honestly and convincingly assure my prospects that they would not see any overpriced houses with me.

### Why pricing the house right in the beginning is so important

This helped me greatly if a buyer suggested that he would like to make an offer on a particular piece of property. I would remind him that all the houses I worked on were fairly priced, and that the chances of an offer being accepted were very slim. I'd go on to say that in a sense I had made his offer for him at the time I took the listing. I could truthfully tell him that I would not permit my sellers to add two or three thousand dollars to the price, expecting to come down when a buyer was found. I could show him where the ridiculous, dangerous and time-wasting game of offer and counter offer had been eliminated.

My records verify that after I had adopted this plan, I seldom had to write a contract for less than the asking price. In my opinion, this is doing it the easy way. When you have the signature of a qualified buyer on a contract for the full price of the house, you have a satisfied buyer, a happy seller, and no problems. How sweet it is!

### If you lose control of the buyer
### you will lose your sale

In spite of all this, I would occasionally have a buyer who still insisted on offering less than the asking price. These sales must not be lost. When this situation occurred I was mindful of the interests of the seller—after all, he would pay my commission. I would use all the persuasion I possessed to convince the buyer to make his offer close to the listed price. I would explain to him that if the offer was too low it would only irritate and anger the seller and greatly reduce the chances of getting ANY offer of less than the full price accepted.

As an example, I would explain that I might have a chance of getting an offer of five hundred dollars less than the full price accepted, and practically no chance with an offer of a thousand dollars less. I would hold at this line as long as possible, but in the end the buyer made the offer on his terms. If I considered it a fair offer I would explain to the buyer that I would do everything in my power to get it accepted, but I would also warn him that I couldn't guarantee acceptance, and that he should be prepared for further negotiations. Since I had indoctrinated him from the beginning with the idea that I worked only with houses that had prices equal to or below the fair market value, I received less than usual resistance later if I had to bring him up to full price.

### Work for the seller when selling the buyer,
### and for the buyer when selling the seller

In the first place, I would not write up an offer unless I personally believed it to be a fair one. Theoretically, the right to refuse any offer belongs to the seller because the property belongs to him. Experience has shown me, however, that an offer too low angers the seller and is a good way to lose both the sale and the listing: therefore, I refused to write up an offer that I did not consider fair and reasonable. This practice definitely helped me make many ADDITIONAL sales.

Once I had done my level best in the interest of the seller and had a fair offer signed by the buyer, I changed hats. Now I must work with equal effort in the interest of the buyer. More accurately, I should say I was now working for the buyer, the seller, and myself.

Presenting an offer to a seller who still believes that his property is priced too low is an adventure not to be attempted unprepared. As described earlier, I had previously cultivated the goodwill, confidence and friendship of my sellers, and that stood me in good stead in the event that I took them an offer below their asking price.

### The disarming psychology of good news

The manner in which I presented the offer depended considerably upon the temperament and personality of my sellers. I would phone and ask to see them for a few minutes concerning their house. In cases where I anticipated very little trouble, as soon as I was inside the door I would greet them with the announcement,

"I have good news for you! I have just sold your house!"

If I had catalogued them properly, when I handed them the sales agreement they would be reluctant to make a big issue of the lower price. We might hang up on the point momentarily, but usually the words "Your house is sold" were far too pleasant for them to argue long over the price. They liked the feeling that their house was sold, and were content to accept it as so.

### Don't walk on stage
### until you have learned your lines

With sellers from whom I expected considerable, even extreme resistance, I used a far more complicated approach. Every step had to be planned. Every thought and every sentence had to be prepared. The answers to anticipated questions and arguments had to be rehearsed.

Presenting offers to sellers gave me many exciting and unforgettable hours. I've been through it dozens and dozens of times over the years, but for reasons of demonstration the method I found successful will be described by a case that happened during my year of a million dollars in sales.

### The cost of a home doesn't necessarily dictate the selling price

To start with, there are many understandable reasons why sellers have difficulty pricing their house to the market. Some of these are:

1. Building a high-cost home in a medium-price neighborhood.
2. After purchasing a home, overimproving it.
3. Buying a home in a transitional neighborhood where encroaching business, industrial concerns, or thoroughfares have downgraded the property.

There are other reasons, but these are the major ones.

### The value of all homes seeks the level of the neighborhood

Fundamentally, this illustration paralleled all other presentations of an offer. Only the conversation and degree of resistance varied. The sellers, Mr. and Mrs. Knight, had built a lovely $35,000 home, but in a $25,000 neighborhood. It was truly outstanding, and other people as well as I repeatedly attempted to convince the Knights to let us list it at a price we felt the market would bring. They refused.

The months went by and for almost a year the house was on the open market. There was no action at all from real estate men. The owners kept a now-faded and weatherbeaten "For Sale" sign on the front lawn, and also ran an occasional newspaper ad, but the high price constantly defeated them.

### When a house sits too long it's a cinch the price is too high

Because it was a lovely custom-built home, I had not forgotten it, and was therefore pleased when Mr. Knight came into the office one day to announce that he was ready to lower his price if I were willing to go to work on selling the property.

There was no doubt that he had every bit of $35,000 in the home, and it wasn't easy to get him to agree to list it below $30,000. But we finally settled on a price of $29,500. Although I still felt this was on the high side, I agreed to do the best I could. Before he left, he stated very clearly that he would not take one dollar less than the price we had agreed upon.

The time had come to start tempering him for the offer I felt sure would be made. I began,

### Any house is only worth what someone is willing to pay for it

"Mr. Knight, it is simply not possible for either you or me to set the price on your home with absolute certainty. In the end, the buyer sets the price on a house, not the seller. Any property, anywhere in the world, is only worth what someone is willing to pay for it. Also," I continued, "there is another rule of real estate which you should be aware of, and it is this: What you pay for a house or what you put into it doesn't *necessarily* have anything to do with what it will sell for. You have asked me to do a job for you, and since I don't make a dime until I make a sale, the degree of my efforts will be in direct ratio to my opinion of your cooperation if I should have to bring to you what I consider a fair offer."

### A diehard seller compounds the problem

He was not impressed. He had reconciled himself to taking a loss—but there was a point beyond which he would not go. As I watched him drive off I thought to myself, What a merry time you and I are going to have if I should get an interested buyer. As it turned out, merry wasn't the word for it—frantic, was more like it.

The following day I visited the Knights. I familiarized myself again with the home, spent some time establishing a friendly relationship with the owners, put MY "For Sale" sign on the lawn, and left. Some six weeks went by and I had not been able to generate much action on the Knights' property. And then it happened.

### Buyers with a strong desire for a specific location will occasionally pay a premium price

Late one afternoon I looked up from my desk and saw a well-dressed, middle-aged couple smiling at me. I hadn't heard them come in. Addressing me from the nameplate on my desk, they said,

"Mr. Gardiner, we're wondering if you have any homes—something fairly nice—in the Redding Lane area."

Did I! I had something more than fairly nice. The Knights lived at 2112 Redding Lane.

We were on our way to that address in short order. During the drive I learned that my prospects were named Wilson, and that Mrs. Wilson had a younger sister who lived in the Knights' neighborhood, which was the main reason they wanted to live there. As we pulled up in front of the house, Mr. Wilson said,

"My wife and I have admired this house many times, but we understand it's priced at $35,000. We have no intention of spending that much for a home."

"That was the price to begin with," I answered. "However, the owners have made a large reduction. I would like to suggest that you look at the home first, and if you are pleased with it, then we'll discuss price."

They agreed, and spent the next hour or more losing their hearts to the charm and beauty of the lovely home. I wanted very much to make this sale to the Wilsons, because they had reason to live in this particular neighborhood and therefore would come closer to paying the asking price than any other prospects I was likely to get.

### A little sympathy mellows a hostile seller

When we were back at the office, I told them the price and expounded at great length on the quality and desirability of the home. Mr. Wilson made the first move when he said they would be willing to pay $26,000 for it. About an hour and a half later, using every persuasive method I ever knew, I obtained their signatures on a purchase contract in the amount of $27,500. I was satisfied. I knew they would not go a dollar higher. I also knew it was a fair offer. I bid them goodnight, assuring them I would report my failure or success with the sellers.

I sat at my desk in the deserted office for probably thirty minutes, thinking over what lay ahead of me, and when I felt I was ready, I called the Knights and said,

"I know it's very late, but I have a matter to discuss with you that I think should be done tonight. May I drop over for a few minutes?"

"Come right over," was the answer.

**Act when you feel the time is right,
but not before**

One of the many talents required to be a top real estate man is the ability to be an actor. For a situation such as I was about to walk into, it is absolutely essential. Well aware that my success would not come from any one profound statement, or any single piece of clever strategy, but rather would result from a combination of many, many little things, I was mentally programmed when the Knights opened the door. I managed to look exhausted. I sounded dead tired when I said,

"Good evening."

When I was invited into the living room, I sank deep into an easy chair exclaiming, "What a night I've had! I'm really beat."

The folded sales agreement was in my hand, purposely, and I knew it had not escaped their attention. They knew whatever I had been doing had something to do with the sale of their house. I added one more comment:

"It's good to relax for a moment."

Mrs. Knight, with womanly concern, asked if I'd like a cup of coffee.

"I could *sure* use one," I replied.

While she attended to the coffee, I struck up a conversation with her husband which had nothing to do with houses, real estate, or contracts. I talked about everything I could think of—news stories in the morning paper, city politics, the weather, baseball, and anything else that occurred to me to keep the conversation going. As I talked, I flourished the contract to emphasize one point or another. Mr. Knight's eyes frequently fastened on the document for a few seconds. Meanwhile, the coffee had arrived and I drank two cups without referring exactly to why I was there.

Mr. Knight was well aware that I held a contract in my hand. He was thinking either, "He has sold our house for full price and knows he will have no trouble getting us to sign the agreement before he goes, otherwise he would be spending his time trying to convince us to take it:" or, "He has a very low offer, and he's afraid to tell us what it is."

### The seller explodes, as expected

Experience had taught me that delaying the presentation of the offer allowed time for the sellers' hopes that their house was sold to grow, and also tempered and mellowed any emotional explosion that they were prepared to make when I first arrived. It was a small advantage, true: but a little edge was all I needed with which to start my presentation. I felt the time had come.

After a short pause to be sure I had their attention, I slowly began to unfold the sales agreement, and while doing so, I said,

"I have sold your house . . . provided that you accept the terms of this agreement."

### The point of contention is the amount
### between the seller's price and the buyer's offer

I handed a copy to each of them: then I sat back to wait.

I was bursting to say a dozen things, but I held my silence and studied Mr. Knight's face as he read the agreement. I knew I was in for trouble when he stopped reading halfway down the paper, then laid it on the coffee table in front of him. He had stopped at the point where the price was given. While he and I sat quietly, Mrs. Knight read the entire agreement.

I let a few seconds pass, then addressed Mr. Knight. "We have a good buyer here; did you notice the amount of his down payment?"

He ignored my question and asked his own. "You don't expect us to take that price for our house, do you?"

"That's why I'm here," I responded.

To say the least, Mr. Knight was angry. The anger was in him ready to come out, and come out it did.

"WE'RE NOT GOING TO GIVE THIS HOUSE AWAY!"

For the next few minutes I heard once again how much it had cost to build the house; how he had watched every brick laid and every nail driven. He enumerated all the additional items they had added, and their cost. He told me that friends of theirs had sold *their* house for more than they, the Knights, were asking. Again he repeated, "We are certainly not going to *give* this house away!" "You might as well tell your buyers if they don't want to pay our price to forget it. We'll keep the house."

He had had his say: now it was my turn. But before I said a word, I picked up both copies of the contract, folded them, and put them in my coat pocket.

### Reducing the difference into digestible quantities

Somewhat wearily, I said, "I'm sorry you're not pleased with this offer. I worked very hard to get it. I did my very best to bring my buyers up to this final figure. One thing I can assure you: they will not go any higher. I brought this offer to you because I honestly believe it is a fair one. I've had a hard day: I am anxious to get home and go to bed, but before I go, I feel I have an obligation to clarify a few points that you've overlooked.

"I don't want you to regret a hasty decision, so please make a mental note of what I'm about to tell you. The Wilsons have offered $27,500 for your home, and that is the figure uppermost in your minds. But . . . what we're really concerned about is that it is two thousand dollars below your asking price, so let's take a close look at that two thousand dollars.

"In spite of your firm stand on your price of $29,500, I can't believe that you would have refused an offer five hundred dollars less, now would you? So we're talking about fifteen hundred dollars. Hold that figure in your mind for a moment.

"Your house has been on the market for months, and this is the first offer you have had. Think of the amount of taxes and insurance, and the interest on your mortgage that you have paid since it went on the market. Let's assume, as I think we can rightfully do, that there will be at least an equal period of time before you get another offer. As you well know, at the very minimum, you will spend an additional five hundred dollars during that time for insurance, interest and upkeep. If you accept this offer, you will save that five hundred dollars.

"Now we have a difference of one thousand dollars. If you choose to continue the anxiety, frustration, and inconvenience of having your house on the market for the sake of one thousand dollars, that's your business. I respectfully tell you you are making a grave economic mistake.

"It is my professional opinion that you have a very fair offer, and

I think you should sign the agreement right now because, when I leave, this offer leaves with me. I don't believe, if you wait six weeks or six months, that you'll get more."

### The seller's last stand

By studying the two people as I talked, I was convinced that Mrs. Knight was ready to capitulate. Not Mr. Knight, however. He gathered his anger and launched into a repetition of his earlier tirade so vehemently that I suddenly KNEW that he, too, was on the verge of giving in. He realized this, also, and it explained why he defended his position so vigorously. I knew I needed only to sit and wait.

It was quite a wait. He was wound up tight. He charged off on matters not at all pertinent to our problem. He crossed the room from chair to chair, sitting only a few moments in each one. He argued long and loud, but he finally ran down. His final statement was a rather weak,

"We'll just hang on a while longer."

I was sure I saw a look of disappointment cross his wife's face.

"Very well," I said, "I've done the best I could, I'm sorry it wasn't enough."

### Closing in for the sale

I crossed over and shook hands with Mr. Knight, thanked his wife for the coffee, and headed for the door. With my hand on the doorknob, I turned to Mr. Knight:

"By the way, I want to wish you luck in your new business."

"What business is that?" he asked.

"The real estate business. You have just become a real estate speculator."

He looked puzzled.

"You've just bought your own house back," I explained, "and you are now speculating that you will get a few hundred dollars more."

"I don't quite follow you," he said.

I took a few steps toward him.

### A crisis created for the seller

"You see, it's like this. A little while ago, I handed you $27,500, and momentarily took your house. You decided you didn't like the deal. You gave me back the $27,500 and took back your house. What you really did was buy your own house back for $27,500, because you believed there was a chance you would get more. That's known as 'speculating' in real estate. I wish you luck, but I honestly don't believe you will have much success."

"Just a minute," he protested, "you've got me confused."

"It's really simple, Mr. Knight. You already have the $27,500. What you are getting ready to do is waste a lot of time and effort, and keep your home and family in an unsettled condition, hoping and wishing to get a few hundred dollars more. I don't believe that will happen. I think you have the highest offer you'll ever get.

"Think for a moment what happens if this speculation venture of yours backfires. Suppose that the next offer, if and when it comes, is less than the one you have now. There is a belief in the real estate business that generally your first offer is your best offer."

### A successful conclusion—just as I planned it

Mr. Knight stood staring at the floor, lost in deep thought. I let him think it over. Finally I said,

"Whether you believe it or not, I've done an exceptionally good job for you people. Why don't you face the facts, quit kidding yourselves, and stop struggling with the impossible? You will be money ahead, have peace of mind and, when you're out from under the emotional strain of this thing, you will realize, as I do now, that you did the wise thing.

"You don't want to be a real estate speculator: you don't want to drag this thing out over additional weeks and months for nothing. For your own sake, listen to my advice. Don't let me leave here with this contract unsigned. You may never get another one as good."

Mr. Knight was listening, but this time he made no response. Mrs. Knight finally spoke up.

"John, I agree with Mr. Gardiner. I think we should sign it."

The time for talking was over. Without a word, I handed the contract to Mr. Knight, and without a word, he signed it.

The man who swore he wouldn't take a dollar less for his property took two thousand less, and I had earned an $825 commission the *hard* way.

### A checklist for closing the seller

1. Work diligently with the buyer to obtain the highest and best sales agreement possible to present to the seller.

2. Greet your sellers with the statement, "YOUR HOUSE IS SOLD— providing you accept the terms of this agreement."

3. Have the agreement in an envelope, folder or briefcase, so that during the time you extract it, separate the copies and hand one to your seller and his wife, you have sufficient time to drive home the information that you have worked long and hard with the buyer, and this is the absolute best you could do.

4. Remain absolutely silent while the agreement is being read.

5. If they voice any objections to the terms, particularly to the price, you must FORCE them to REFUSE the offer. (Occasionally you will be surprised to learn that they intended to accept the offer, but wanted to let off a little steam first.)

6. When they have definitely stated in so many words that they ARE refusing your offer, you can then proceed to sell the seller. (You must not assume he is refusing the offer: he must SAY SO. Then you're in the groove to proceed.)

7. You now give him back his house, and take back the amount of money mentioned in the offer.

   a. Gather up all copies of the agreement. Hold them in your hand.
   b. Tell the sellers you're sorry the offer was not satisfactory to them and that you had worked very hard to bring them one you thought was very fair.
   c. Slowly and silently replace the contract in the envelope or brief case.
   d. As you stand up to leave, thank them for their consideration: then say, "I really thought I had your house sold; maybe I'll do better next time."

8. You drop the bomb. Make a casual comment—

    a. "I'll bet you didn't expect to buy a house today, did you?"
    or b. "I guess you realize you just became real estate specu-
    lators."

Their answer will be something like, "We don't understand what you mean." When that happens, then you SELL. Tell them that when they refused the offer they bought their own house back, and in doing so became real estate speculators. They are now hoping— no guarantee—just hoping, that in a few days or weeks, or some- times months, they will get a few hundred dollars more for their property.

Assume total control of the situation. Review forcibly all the reasons that convinced you that you brought them a fair offer. Conclude your selling by telling them,

"You don't want to become real estate speculators; it just isn't worth it. Why don't you sign this agreement and your house will be sold!"

Before they can answer, quickly hand them the agreement, but this time, hand them your pen too.

You are through selling, so be very quiet, and let them think over what you said. The next sound you'll hear will be the scratch of your pen on paper.

### Points to remember

1. In real estate you sell twice during each sale: the buyer, and then the seller.
2. The BEST time to sell the seller is when you list the property.
3. If you don't work with overpriced property, you will have a few problems with offers.
4. If a seller refuses a fair offer, he has bought his own house back, and becomes a real estate speculator.
5. Until the SELLER is sold, there is no sale.

# CHAPTER 15

# AN ACT OF KINDNESS LED TO A CHAIN OF FOURTEEN SALES

---

I gave gentle and considerate attention to the problems of a widowed lady who needed help in selling her home. It was a small enough act on my part, but it was to be directly responsible for a chain of sales totalling over THREE HUNDRED THOUSAND DOLLARS!

## A TIME FOR KINDNESS

When people are suddenly confronted with the necessity of buying or selling a home, they are often beset with worry and the fear of being cheated or taken advantage of. This fear is very real and very strong and should not be dismissed or ignored. If you do ignore it, you are not true to your profession and you will not earn the income of which you are capable.

During the time I was trying to determine what made a few salesmen stand out far above the others, I found that there were two traits characteristic of all of them: one was honesty, the other, kindness. I soon learned why they placed such value on kindness. I discovered that being kind and considerate generated confidence. When I had the confidence of both the buyer and the seller, I usually made a sale. In many cases it gave me a psychological exclusive and, what's equally important, it led to referrals. Rather than attempt to define the special type of kindness applicable to the real estate business, I have selected from many experiences a particular case which I think dramatically demonstrates its power in this field.

## I COUNTERACTED MY CLIENT'S FEARS WITH KINDNESS AND WAS AWARDED WITH A REFERRAL THAT WAS TO PRODUCE THOUSANDS OF DOLLARS IN COMMISSIONS

At first glance it was a simple matter of listing a home for a lady who lived alone. If I were successful in selling it, there was a pretty fair chance that I would be able to sell her another one. There was nothing unusual about this, but my association with her was to be responsible for the longest series of linked sales I had ever made. They totaled fourteen.

When I arrived at Mrs. James' home to write up the listing, I found her to be a diminutive, highly nervous, and very much frightened person. Because of this, we sat down for a get-acquainted visit. We had to arrive at a meeting of the minds. I wanted to dispel her fears, develop her confidence in me, and convince her that I was a competent, honest, and considerate real estate man who would not let her interests be neglected.

To accomplish all this convincingly, I had to mean what I said. After we finished our conversation, she appeared to be considerably relieved, yet a little of her apprehension was still apparent. I took the information necessary to complete the listing, and left her with the promise that I would work hard in her behalf. Words are cheap. Up to this point, all I had given her were words. Some acts of kindness should follow, and I laid the plans to perform them.

I was conscientiously concerned about the peace of mind and well-being of Mrs. James, who desperately needed someone whom she could trust and rely on to help her in a matter about which she admittedly was ignorant and, therefore, vulnerable. I decided to become that someone.

***Keep in touch with the seller
is the first step to a sale***

I visited with her either by phone or at her home at least once a day during the time her house was on the market. I advised her beforehand of newspaper ads on her home and gave her the names of people with whom I had discussed her property. I made an effort to discover mutual friends, and brought them into our conversations, and tried to broaden the variety of topics that would cement our relationship.

We talked about her sons in college, her job as a secretary, mutual church activities, raising flowers, trips we had taken: in short, we visited as old friends, which we had become in a surprisingly brief time. She came to place her trust in me and my advice, and not for all the money in the world would I have failed that trust.

### Conversion of a "sleeper" into a hot listing

When I suggested some alterations be made to the appearance of her property, she was readily agreeable. Her home was an older, brick Cape Cod. She had kept the interior spick-and-span but, because there was no man on the premises, the exterior of the house and the landscaping showed considerable neglect. The impressive appearance and charm characteristic of many older brick homes was lost to view behind overgrown shrubbery and tangled vines. My plan was to trim this overgrowth to a proper height. When this was done, it exposed weatherbeaten wooden shutters, but when these were covered with a few coats of white paint, our product was ready for sale.

Almost before the paint was dry we had a buyer. The newly revealed charm of the old home caught the eye of a lady passing by in her car. She said she had been watching for many months for a home of just this kind to come on the market.

### Confidence once planted must be cultivated

When the papers were drawn and signed, Mrs. James was pleased, but also frightened, because now she needed a home for herself. In the ensuing days I continued the practice of stopping by for a few moments each evening. She responded again and seemed to stop worrying while I searched diligently for exactly the right property for her.

I called her one evening to tell her I thought I'd found her next home, and her response was,

"Wonderful! That's a big worry off my mind."

She indicated such confidence in my selection that she was almost ready to buy without seeing the house. There's no doubt that this enviable position of trust was created because I took the time to dispel her fears, to reassure her, and to be her friend. To me, this is the kindness required to be rated a top real estate man.

## THE REVERBERATING REFERRAL

After I had seen to it that Mrs. James was satisfactorily settled in her new home, my contacts with her became less frequent. Many months went by, and then one afternoon an incident took place which involved me, although I did not learn of it until some time later.

### Kindness returned tenfold

Mrs. James was the private secretary of the owner and president of a large manufacturing concern who often ventured into large real estate investments and development. His son-in-law had considerable wealth and equal prominence, and together they planned to construct a large business complex. On this particular afternoon the two men were having a meeting to discuss the land acquisition for the development. Mrs. James was present.

They had decided upon a centrally located parcel of ground, which had eight owners. There were seven dwellings and one vacant lot. To acquire this property, which encompassed an entire block, would be no small endeavor. After they had settled on the site, they were discussing how best to purchase it, and one of the men said,

"If we only knew a real estate man we could trust."

Mrs. James more than repaid me for what kindness I had shown her when she had the courage to say,

"I know one you can trust," and gave them my name.

It was the start of an association which was to bring fourteen sales and earn over NINE THOUSAND DOLLARS in commissions for me. A pretty good convincer that kindness pays.

## THE COMPLEX TASK OF CONVINCING
## UNMOTIVATED OWNERS TO BECOME SELLERS

An evaluation of the task at hand clearly revealed that if the owners were not approached in the proper sequence, I would have more problems than I might be able to handle. Each purchase had to be negotiated separately, but if any owner refused to sell the whole plan would fail. It was like a pile of jackstraws—which one should I touch first?

There were eight contiguous lots. One was vacant, and seven contained old dwellings, four of them occupied by the owners, two rented to tenants, and one inhabited by two elderly ladies whose nephew owned the house. The developer had left it up to me to negotiate the best price I could on each property. Because most of the residents had been there for many, many years, I expected some unwilling, and some belligerent sellers. I got both.

### *Where 90 percent success was*
### *tantamount to failure*

My developer pointedly reminded me in the beginning that none of the properties would be of any value to him unless he could purchase all of them. He was willing to gamble that I would be able to obtain all eight.

There were two things in our favor. Many years before, this street, which was close to the center of town, had been rezoned to permit the type of development in which we were interested: secondly, because of this my buyer could afford to pay more than these antiquated buildings were worth as homes. The higher prices would enable the owners to purchase far better homes in nicer neighborhoods. Subsequent events were to bring out that my biggest problem was the owners' sentimental attachment to the old homestead.

Since I had to start somewhere, I decided to contact the owner of the vacant lot.

### The over-anxious seller

When the square footage, expected return, and building cost of any type of income property have been determined, it is a simple matter to calculate the amount that it is economically feasible to expend for the landsite. This we had done, and I had a fair idea of what we could pay for each property.

A unique situation developed where the vacant lot was concerned. To us, a vacant lot was more desirable than one with a building on it, since the cost of razing the building would be eliminated. However, the owner of the lot believed that since there was no building on the lot, it was less valuable than the adjacent properties and, of course, under ordinary circumstances this would be true.

Of the total amount of money we hoped would be sufficient to purchase the entire block, I determined a pro-rated share to offer Mrs. Gleason for her vacant lot. The very day that I intended to present my offer, her lawyer called to say that his client understood I had someone interested in buying land on First Street. If this were so, she would be willing to sell her lot for $6,500. I replied that if he would draft the sales agreement in that amount, I would take it to my buyer.

The $6,500 was one thousand dollars LESS than I had intended to offer. We had made our first purchase.

### The seller who wouldn't stand still

There was a very large and very old house on the lot next to Mrs. Gleason's. It had been converted into a two-family residence, with one family renting the upstairs, another the downstairs. The owner was an oldtimer in the county, and owned and operated a large farm eight or ten miles out of the city. I decided he was the one I would approach next.

**The first evasion.—**I found him operating a tractor in a soybean field. When he pulled abreast of where I was standing, he stopped the tractor but didn't shut off the engine, nor did he give any indication that he intended to. Almost yelling to make myself heard over the roar of the tractor, I introduced myself and said,

"Mr. Powell, I'm here in regard to your property on First Street. I have a party interested in buying it."

"Not for sale," he shouted.

In the blink of an eye, he had the tractor in gear and was headed back across the field. My guess was that I had twenty minutes before he would be back at my end again. By that time I'd better have something prepared to attract this old farmer's attention. I thought I had it, and was ready for him when once again he came to a stop.

He beat me to the punch when he yelled, "Haven't got time to talk right now!"

**His refuse-and-run tactic.**—He let in the clutch and was gone again. I was more than a little irritated as I stood there, knee-deep in soybeans, watching Mr. Powell pull out of shouting distance.

**Climbing aboard to the problem.**—I had no intention of leaving. I had to figure out a way to make the old gentleman stand still and listen for a few minutes. Then I had an idea. Maybe he would listen if he didn't have to stop. As he whirled around to make his return trip, I walked to meet him. He paid no attention to me whatever. Timing my pace to the speed of the tractor, I stepped onto the tie bar, put one foot on the gear housing, and leaned against the fender.

**The negotiating power of dollars.**—We rode this way a little while and then I yelled in his ear,

"Would you take fifty thousand dollars for your First Street property?"

He gave no indication that he had heard me, but in another moment when we reached the end of the field he stopped the tractor, turned off the engine, and asked,

"What did you say?"

"I said, 'Would you take fifty thousand dollars for your First Street property?'"

"Certainly I would," he responded.

"Fine," I said, "then it *is* for sale. All we have to do is settle on the price."

He had a friendly smile, and he turned it on full force. We climbed down and sought the shade of a tree, where we proceeded with our price discussion. Mr. Powell admitted that his building was badly in need of repair, but said that he simply didn't have the time to take care of it.

**Reaching for the double sale.**—I said that my buyer would pay cash, and that if he were interested in reinvesting his money in income property, I had two new four-unit, brick apartment buildings, side by side. The proceeds of his sale would be more than an adequate down payment, and he could mortgage the rest. The rental revenue would make the mortgage payments, pay all the expenses, and give him a very handsome cash flow, or net spendable return. Also, the depreciation factor would give him additional tax cover. He was interested.

"Will you sell your building for twenty thousand dollars?" I asked.

"No, but I will take thirty thousand."

We soon arrived at a handshaking figure of $26,500. By the time I reached my car, Mr. Powell was once again halfway across his soybean field.

I returned that evening with the sales agreement for Mr. and Mrs. Powell to sign, and when that was taken care of, I spent two of the most enjoyable hours of my life sitting in the living room of their old farm home, surrounded by furnishings of many generations past, and visiting with these two fine old people. When I left I was richer in more ways than one.

As far as the apartment buildings were concerned, the Powells bought not one, but both of them. It proved to be an excellent investment, and I'm willing to wager they still own both buildings today. The price of the two apartment buildings totalled over $100,000.

On my First Street project, I was now ready for—

### The shrewd investor

Mr. and Mrs. Silverthorne owned the best of the seven houses, located at one end of the block. They were the next ones I approached. They were almost my undoing. They were also the only ones I had to give up on, and return to later. Mr. Silverthorne was a large, soft-spoken man, but a shrewd investor and judge of human character.

When I started on this project, I was determined that anything I told the property owners would be the truth. I did not intend to use pressure, threats, or coercion. I believed I could convince any of them that it was their good fortune to have the opportunity to sell an older home in a business area for an amount sufficient to purchase a better home in a residential neighborhood.

**The seller had the diversionary tactics of a poker player.** Mr. Silverthorne believed that he could not only do this, but also realize a fat profit if he played his cards right. It was quite an experience to spend an evening with him. He announced that he knew the identity of the man who was buying up the First Street property, and also what was going to be built on it. One day he would divulge that Mr. X was going to buy it and build a high-rise apartment building, the next day he was sure Mr. Y was the buyer, and would erect a medical center. Another time he announced that an architect he knew was doing the designing, and that a Mr. Z was the purchaser and would put up a large shopping center.

I couldn't get him to understand that it was immaterial who bought the property or what he intended to do with it. I asked him to set a price on his house and let me submit it to my client. I visited him day after day, and our negotiations were getting nowhere.

There were times when he told me he had definitely decided not to sell at all: other times he said he would sell if he could get his price, but he wouldn't name a figure. Finally, when I was about to give up, and I think he sensed it, he said he would take $50,000. This was at least $20,000 too much for his property. I replied that his price bordered on the ridiculous, but that I would take it to my buyer. Then I went next door to visit the Vernons and open negotiations with them.

Every day, during the next ten days, my car could be seen parked somewhere on First Street. I'm sure the Silverthornes knew this, and I'm also sure every day they expected me to drop in, but I didn't. Finally the suspense became too great, and Mr. Silverthorne called me.

"What did your man think of our price?" was his question.

"It's so far out of line, Mr. Silverthorne, that my client thinks we should drop your property. He believes that possibly he can get by without your property, since you have the last house on the block. He's having the firm which is engineering the layout look into it."

This was true—it *was* possible to do without the Silverthorne property, but we would much prefer to have it.

**Another form of "creating a crisis."** Mr. Silverthorne was now faced with the question, did we mean it, or were we bluffing? If we had to have his property, and he held out, he could force us to pay close to his asking price. If we didn't need it, he would not only lose the amount we *were* willing to pay, but he would also wind up owning a house on the edge of a business complex, which would then be difficult to sell at any price.

I told him we should definitely know our position in about three days. Mr. Silverthorne was a poker player to the end.

"Fine," he said. "We'll wait to hear from you. By the way, we have another party interested in buying our property. If it goes through, I'll let you know right away."

Mr. Silverthorne was doing a little bluffing on his own. Of course, you never can be one hundred percent sure, and I'll admit I was relieved when he decided to play it safe three days later. He phoned me to ask,

"What's the best price your client will pay for our property?"

I quoted what I thought was a very fair figure. He hesitated for a few seconds, then said,

"We'll take it."

We now owned three properties, with five to go. Incidentally, much of the work I did on the First Street project was in the evening after regular working hours. My day-by-day selling activities went on as usual.

### The elderly sellers who feared the advent of progress

I was distressed to learn how frightened Mr. and Mrs. Vernon were when I first visited their home. They were in their eighties. In 1916, the year they were married, they had moved into their house on First Street. Mr. Vernon could now walk only with great difficulty. His wife, a tiny wisp of a thing, was rapidly losing her eyesight. I'm sure they felt that the familiar walls of the old home where they had lived for over forty years provided them with the protection and comfort they so needed in their old age. Now, all at once, their feeling of security was threatened. Rumors had reached their ears that power shovels and giant graders were coming and they would have to move, which they dreaded.

Even though they knew I had something to do with what they considered an approaching disaster, they very graciously invited me in when I came to see them. As quickly and sincerely as I could, I set about to remove the fears gripping the worried old couple, by assuring them that as long as I had anything to do with it, no effort would be made to pressure them into selling. I advised them not to sell if what I had to offer did not improve their position considerably. All I asked was that they listen to my proposition and then make their own decision. They were to have all the time they wanted to make up their minds, and if they should decide to sell, I promised to help them find a home better than the one they now lived in, and to see to it that they were assisted in every way in making the move. I said I'd be happy to work with their lawyer or banker or anyone else they wanted to call in to look after their interests, and that above all, I would have nothing to do with negotiations that would harm, inconvenience, or upset them in any way.

**Confidence honestly earned.** I think they believed I meant what I said, because I did! This was the first of many visits to their home, each one more pleasant than the last. They loved to recount delightful stories of their early life. They had a fascinated listener, and more than once we neglected to discuss the sale of their property at all. Even today, when I think of little Mrs. Vernon, I think of lilacs, fresh-baked pies, and ruby glassware monogrammed in gold. I won their confidence, born of a friendship that grew during our many evening visits.

**Start of the expeditionary thinking.** One evening they said to me,

"We haven't been more than a few blocks from home for years. We don't know what kind of homes are for sale. Would you take us out tomorrow and show us two or three?"

What fun we had the next several days! They were caught up in the excitement of house hunting. Although it was a painful ordeal for them to get in and out of the car and in and out of houses, we managed to see a half dozen of the better small homes on the market. They liked two in particular. One was a brick, ranch-style home, the other a cedar-shingled cottage. Their ultimate decision was to buy both. They rented the brick home and moved into the cottage. The amount of money that we paid them for their house made this possible.

I visited them a time or two in their new home. They were happy and cheerful and, I thought, a little younger. The frightened ones no longer were.

This was the halfway point, and a few months had gone by.

**The detective work needed to
locate an out-of-town owner**

The other house occupied by tenants was owned by Mr. Pickrell, a widower. Everyone seemed to know Mr. Pickrell, but no one knew where to locate him. The tenants paid their rent to a local bank: the bank, in turn, paid the taxes and insurance. At first I wasn't concerned—I thought certainly a man who owned property could be located somehow, but the more I searched the more I became convinced that I had a problem.

Old friends had lost track of him. It appeared he had no relatives and even the bank offered very little help. I had played detective before, and it was just a matter of finding a clue that would lead me to the elusive Mr. Pickrell. By talking to some of the oldtimers around town, I discovered that my quarry was from a small town in the northern part of the state. I had already invested nearly three weeks in my search, so I decided to speed up things by leaving early one morning for the eighty-mile drive to the village of North Greenfield.

I reached the small farming community a little before noon, and soon found many people who knew Mr. Pickrell, but none who had seen him for years or had an idea of his present whereabouts. One old gentleman finally furnished me with my first clue: he recalled that some years back Mr. Pickrell's sister had died and was buried in the local cemetery.

My next stop was the office of the funeral home. Sure enough, a search of the records showed that Mr. Pickrell had paid the funeral expenses of his sister, and gave his address in Milwaukee. When I returned to my office that evening, I attempted to get his telephone number through the information operator, but there was no Pickrell at that address. I was no closer than I had been twelve hours earlier.

**Sometimes it pays to sit down somewhere and THINK.** Then I had an idea, and if it worked out as I thought it might, my search would be over. I dialed Western Union, and sent a telegram to Mr. Pickrell at the address in Milwaukee. Then I went home to await developments.

The next morning at the office I received a call from Western

Union telling me that in the attempt to deliver the telegram the messenger found no one living at the address, but he had inquired of the neighbors, as I hoped he would, and obtained the new address where Mr. Pickrell had recently moved. They read it to me and asked if they should forward the wire. I thanked them and said no, because Mr. Pickrell now lived less than a fifteen-minute drive from my office.

In about that length of time I was ringing his doorbell. I told him the nature of my business, and he was congenial and receptive. It took three weeks to find him, and thirty minutes to sell him.

### The belligerent sellers

Mr. and Mrs. Rawlins were the "against" type of people. They were against taxes, teenagers, additional schools, apartment houses, charity, dogs, and real estate men. And they were particularly against rich men who wanted to "steal" their home and throw them out in the street.

There was no welcome mat outside their front door. I think the only reason they talked to me at all was that I was a target at which they could direct the bitterness and vindictiveness in which they were so enveloped. They had an overpowering desire to get even with all the fancied injustices they believed surrounded them. It didn't take me long to decide that if I were able to get the Rawlins to sell, it would be because they believed they were getting revenge on someone or something by doing so.

**If they won't come over to your side, go over to theirs.** One way to take the wind out of the sails of argumentative people is to agree with them. So, agree with them I did. I agreed that their taxes were terribly high, and told them of a nice area where they could move to, just outside the city limits, and their taxes would be almost 50 percent less. I finally got them to understand that due to the age and condition of their house, it was really not worth very much if resold for a residence. I explained that *here* was a chance to get a nice chunk of a rich man's money, because he needed their land for business usage.

They calmed down a little and began to do some serious think-ing. They agreed to sell after I showed them a home with a few acres of land around it. I told them that some day the city would grow out to them, and they could sell at a profit. With my proposition they stood a good chance of making a profit twice.

Mr. and Mrs. Rawlins were against almost everything except making a profit.

### The owner whose business was
### real estate speculation

Mr. Johnson had owned his property on First Street for a very short time. He made it very firm, clear, and final that he would not sell. He wasn't interested in a better home; he wasn't interested in a profit; my best arguments brought only a big smile and a negative shake of his head.

I tried the old trick that I'd used on Mr. Powell—"Would you take fifty thousand dollars for your property?"

"No," he said, "I wouldn't, because you wouldn't pay it."

Finally, in desperation, I asked, "Why won't you sell, Mr. Johnson?"

"Because," he answered, "I didn't buy this property to sell. I like it here."

"But there's a large business complex coming into the area," I argued.

"That's okay," he answered. "Let 'em build around me."

It appeared that I had finally run up against a brick wall. Mr. Johnson was immovable. There is no doubt that he caused me to lose a few hours' sleep. I still believed there was a key to the problem, and I had to find it. I continued to visit him occasionally, and he said to me one night,

"I'm sorry, George, I know this means a lot to you, but it's simply not to my best interest to sell."

There was a tiny clue. His reference to his 'best interest' was the first indication of any kind of a specific reason why he wouldn't sell. In the course of the many hours of our conversations I had learned that he had speculated in real estate for many years, and that his personal wealth was far greater than anyone would suspect.

I probed and parried and argued gently, but to no avail. I went home that night completely stymied. I thought about it until my head ached, trying to remember similar cases in the past for a guide.

**There are great advantages, for some people, in trading properties.** Suddenly it came to me. If he wouldn't sell, maybe he would TRADE! I literally spun the dial on the telephone.

"Mr. Johnson, if I had a nice piece of income property, would you consider trading your house for it?"

"I might," he answered, "in fact, for a good income property, I'd be very much interested."

What a relief! We had a duplex listed, and it was a simple matter for my client to buy it and trade it to Mr. Johnson for his house. This is precisely what happened.

I had used the wrong bait: Mr. Johnson was a trader, not a seller.

### The owner who put a dollar value on everything, including sentiment

I was seven-eighths of the way. The only property left to acquire belonged to a bachelor named Evans, and it was occupied by his two elderly aunts. If I thought I'd had any trouble up to now, it was nothing compared to the trouble I had with Mr. Evans.

He was a small, nervous man, an impeccable dresser, and looked every inch the banker that he was. His own residence was an old, Victorian home, the interior of which reflected the orderliness and formality of the meticulous man who lived there. I arrived at his front door just as he finished his evening meal, and he invited me into the cool darkness of his old-fashioned living room. I explained as fully as possible the reasons behind my visit, and quoted him the very liberal amount that my client was willing to pay him for his property.

He took no time at all to consider my proposal: he rejected it immediately.

### The clue I missed—almost everything's for sale, at a price

"That's the old home place," he said. "My father built that house himself, back in the early 1900's. My sisters and I grew up there. When I inherited it a few years ago I turned it over to my father's two sisters to use. As long as I live, it will be their home. So there it is: the property is not for sale and won't be as long as either of my aunts are living."

With that, the ball was back in my hands, and I didn't know what to do with it. I knew he didn't need the money, and I also knew that a suggestion to relocate two dear old aunts would be impatiently rejected. And how could I overcome sentiment for the old homestead?

As it turned out, Mr. Evans was a far better salesman than I was. I bought his story—he didn't buy mine—and by doing so I brought many anxious hours on myself. I couldn't originate a single logical argument to convince this man to change his mind, so I decided to go home and think about it.

For the next few days I nearly wore out my brain coming up with new and different propositions. Each day I believed I had a winner, and each evening I would rush over to present it. Mr. Evans was very cordial: he would listen quietly and respectfully, then slowly shake his head. I would leave, deflated and a little discouraged, but the next night I would be back with another inspired proposition.

### The owner knew he could convert the property to cash any time

One of my brainstorms was that my client would purchase a lot in a nice neighborhood and pay all the costs of moving the old home, and would still give him a good price for the vacated lot. Another time I proposed that we pay all the expenses of the two ladies for the rest of their lives in a luxurious new retirement home situated a few miles away. On a third occasion, after these two approaches failed, I tried a different tack. I appealed to his economic nature. I went so far as to point out the injustice to his heirs for him to pass on a dilapidated, almost worthless building. I was offering him the opportunity to convert this property into cash, which he could use to purchase a modern brick duplex, adding substantially to his estate. This plan also failed.

### There is no such thing as a problem without a solution

About the wildest suggestion I had, which even brought a smile from Mr. Evans, was that we build a duplicate of the house nearby, using as much material from the old house as possible to preserve the sentiment and familiarity. Mr. Evans always said no, but nothing more.

Not a clue to the problem could I find. I began to believe that I was whipped, and that my client's giant project would never be a reality. But, with the firm belief that there is no such thing as a problem without an answer, I kept trying.

One Saturday afternoon I persuaded Mr. Evans' lawyer to meet with us to see if a satisfactory way couldn't be found to consummate the sale I needed so desperately. Mr. Evans made no suggestions or comments other than to reject all propositions that we put to him. When we parted about six o'clock, my discouragement had reached a new low.

### A simple solution; if you have to have it you offer more money

On the way home I remembered there was one thing I hadn't tried. I made a U-turn and in minutes I was standing at Mr. Evans' front door.

"Mr. Evans, would you sell your property if we raised our offer three thousand dollars?"

Without a moment's hesitation, he said, "Yes, I would."

Sentiment for the old homestead had its price. Later on, he moved the two aunts into the big house with him. Why he didn't simply say he wanted more money for the house, I will never know. That was just his way of doing things. I did it the hard way—I forgot to keep it simple. Nevertheless, it was finished.

Here's a brief review of the chain of sales to pinpoint the techniques used:

1. *The over-anxious seller.* This one came about with no effort, like the free square in the center of a bingo board. Since I had already determined the land value, it was possible to immediately accept the amount stated in the offer to sell.

2. *The seller who wouldn't stand still.* I applied one of the oldest techniques in the world here. When an owner says a possession of his is not for sale, ask him very seriously if he would take a half million dollars for it. Although he knows you're joking, he will, of course, say yes, if you press for an answer. Thus you have determined that it is for sale—all that's left is to settle on a price.

It should be noted that during this sale or any other one, for that matter, I had no intention of being put off. I had to get the man's attention, so I climbed aboard the moving tractor. To obtain my objective, I would wade a river or climb up to a rooftop, and I've done both.

3. *The shrewd investor.* You will recognize the "Creating a Crisis" technique used on Mr. Silverthorne. After I had offered to buy his property at a fair market price, I later told him I thought we could get along without it—I took away from him an opportunity to sell his property. In doing so I created a crisis. He had to figure out if I were bluffing. He decided not to take the gamble.

4. *The elderly sellers.* This was the truth-and-tenderness technique, well laced with kindness. Kindness is an antidote for fear.

5. *The out-of-town owner.* Here was the time for perseverance and ingenuity. A real estate man must be many things, and one of them is to be a fair detective. The search was the perseverance: the telegram was the ingenuity.

6. *The belligerent sellers.* The old faithful method of allowing people to sell themselves did the trick here. All I had to do was to feed them what they wanted to hear, and in doing so I let them become the salesman. They soon sold themselves.

7. *The owner whose business was real estate speculation.* This sale needed perseverance, and probing questions. In real estate there is an ANSWER to every PROBLEM. Often the people you are dealing with know the answer but won't tell you: they make you dig for it. To a speculator, trading property has great advantages tax-wise. That was the answer I had to dig for.

8. *The owner who put a dollar value on everything.* There was so simple an answer to this one that I almost overlooked it. A rule of real estate is that any buyer will buy if the price is LOW enough and any seller will sell if the price is HIGH enough. When you are struggling with a problem sale, try a price adjustment for clearing the air. If that *is* the answer, try the split-the-difference technique. Whatever you do, just *don't* give up!

Don't overlook the method "If I—Will you." In this instance, *If I* can get the buyer to raise his offer, *will you* sell?

In almost a year to the day I delivered the last of the properties to my client and fulfilled the confidence Mrs. James had shown when she recommended me. I had made a total of fourteen sales that earned me just under TEN THOUSAND DOLLARS in commissions.

### Points to remember

1. Kindness is a "gentle and considerate behavior" that will put dollars in your pocket.
2. Don't commingle confidences.
3. If it appears to be something no one else would do, do it.
4. When you have earned someone's confidence, you have a psychological exclusive.
5. If your prospect wants to trade, you double the commission you've made.
6. Usually the more complex the problem the simpler the answer.
7. If you let up or give up your efforts to bring buyer and seller together, you have sabotaged your very reason for existence as a real estate man.

# CHAPTER 16

# AN ANGRY SALESMAN WHO TOSSED A SALE IN MY LAP

---

Doug was angry because he had lost a sale. His anger cost him a NINE HUNDRED DOLLAR commission. He then missed another sale on the rebound. Doug's anger caused him to forget that when a house is SOLD, the SELLER becomes a BUYER.

Unreasonable anger robs a man of every faculty he needs to be a salesman. Professional salesmen use controlled anger to make sales: amateur salesmen allow uncontrolled anger to cost them sales. To be a top salesman, be alert to any change or any development from any occurrence whatsoever. The change in circumstance can happen in a split second—you must react equally as fast. Your reaction must be unemotional, keyed to the business you are in. This is an important part of the mental attitude that will help you sell a MILLION DOLLARS worth of real estate in the next twelve months.

If someone's going to be angry, let it be the other guy. He may toss a sale to you, as Doug did to me.

### AN ANGRY SALESMAN CAN'T THINK

Doug was what I would call a scientific real estate man. He went according to the book, so to speak: he was like a robot with a smile. Doug had two problems: he couldn't go beyond his memorized sales technique, and he had an explosive temper.

One afternoon these handicaps tossed a nice commission right into my pocket. Our office had listed an exceptionally nice, colonial style bi-level, which Doug had shown to prospects of his shortly after we listed it. They were very much pleased with it and, I believe, fully intended to buy it. But, they decided to think it over.

**They probably didn't buy
because they weren't asked to**

Doug was on the phone every day talking with them. They discussed each square foot of the property. They had Doug running down all sorts of information: the exact type of insulation, the B.T.U. rating of the furnace, the weight of the roof shingles, when the house was last painted—every day there were more questions, and every day Doug was doing research. A week went by, and not once did Doug attempt to apply any method or technique of closing.

And then the inevitable happened, and it happened at a time when I was at my desk. Doug's phone rang, and it was the owners of the bi-level calling to say that another broker had just sold their house. Doug hung up the phone and hit the ceiling.

He was furious. He belabored his bad luck. He was sure that today was the day his prospects had intended to buy the house. He was one mad guy, getting madder by the minute. He finally stormed out of the office, got into his car, and drove off.

**He forgot that when the house is sold,
the seller often becomes a buyer**

An angry man can't think, and Doug was angry. I wasn't. I picked up the phone, called the owner of the bi-level and, introducing myself, said,

"Mr. Holliday, I'm calling to say that I'm happy for you that your home is sold."

"Thank you," he replied, "I'm sorry Mr. Rainey didn't make the sale. He worked so hard—we felt sure he would."

Evading that subject, I went on, "If I remember correctly, at the time we listed your property you said your intentions were to buy a larger home on the north side."

"That's right. In fact, we intend to look around a little in that area ourselves today, and the broker who sold our house is going to show us some homes there tomorrow."

### A motivated buyer, the right home,
### and the time necessary to bring them together

What a beautiful situation! As sweet as apple pie! Here was a couple with a pocketful of money who had to have a home, knew what they wanted, and where they wanted it. And no one was going near them until tomorrow!

In my selected top 10 percent you can be sure that I had a few outstanding homes on the north side. I told the Hollidays just enough about them to stir their interest. Once they were in my car, they were under my control. We headed toward the north side to inspect any and all properties I chose to show them. By the time the sun went down, Mr. and Mrs. Holliday were once again home-owners, and I had EIGHT HUNDRED AND SEVENTY DOLLARS in *my* pocket.

Poor Doug! While he was complaining about the loss of one sale he lost another.

Contact a seller the minute you learn his home is sold. He may be ripe to buy another one.

## OTHER RICOCHET SALES

Mildred Graham was a worthy competitor. She was an attractive, competent, energetic real estate saleslady whom I admired very much. However, one day she complained too long and too loud, and her prospect wound up in my office.

Millie had shown homes to Mr. Birely all one morning, but he rejected each of them for one reason or another. With each rejection Millie's temperature rose a degree. Finally the noon hour arrived, and she asked her prospect to join her for lunch. He refused, but agreed to meet her in about an hour.

### Keep your words sweet—
### you may have to eat them

A little later, as Millie was eating with friends in a coffee shop nearby, she brought up the subject of Mr. Birely. In rather colorful language and in a most unkind manner, she described to her companions the experience she had had that morning with the "impossible" and "unreasonable" Mr. Birely. She wound up by saying,

"I almost hope I never see him again at the office."

She never did. Millie wasn't aware that Mr. Birely was seated back to back with her in the next booth.

### A ricochet prospect

Later in the day Mr. Birely stopped in my office. It was very noticeable that he was not in a good mood. He described the type of house he wanted in a brusque, no-nonsense tone of voice. After a few qualifying questions I decided to show him a house which I believed was one of the best buys we'd had in many months.

When we arrived at the property, Millie was just getting into her car with some other prospects to whom she had shown the house. As we turned into the walk, she shouted,

"Mr. Birely won't like that house, George, the rooms are too small!"

**I suspect Millie had been shotgun selling and missed the RIGHT house.** Then she pulled away. Millie had misread this man somewhere, because not only did he like the house, but he bought it. It was later, when I asked him if he knew Millie, since she had called him by name, that he told me all that occurred earlier in the day. Millie forgot you don't start selling until the prospect says no, and her lapse of memory enriched me by ONE THOUSAND AND EIGHTY DOLLARS.

### I LEARNED BY LOSING

It seems that I had to learn everything the hard way. One day I received an inquiry from a national concern that wanted to purchase some land to construct a branch plant. I researched the area thoroughly, and located a number of parcels which would serve their purpose. I thought one piece in particular was so good that they would be downright foolish to pass it up. I submitted various parcels, along with my written opinion of the one I thought would be the best for them to buy.

Then I waited for them to appear at my office with check in

hand. I believed I had done a good job, and I was extremely confident that they would purchase the land I recommended. But they didn't.

I could hardly believe it when I learned that they had chosen a parcel submitted by another real estate office. I was indignant, angry and very disappointed. I had lost a nice sale. I bemoaned my bad luck, and questioned the intelligence of the company representative who made the purchase. My day was ruined. I turned off my brain and left the office to wade chin-deep in gloom for the rest of the day—the reaction of a rank amateur.

### Senseless anger prohibits creative selling

At the office one of the men did what I should have done. He got on the phone, located the representative of the company, and obtained the name of the man who was being sent to town to oversee the construction, and eventually to be the plant manager. He made an appointment to meet the gentleman, later sold him a very expensive home and ultimately, through this connection, found houses for a number of the company personnel as they were transferred in.

While I was wasting time at the wailing-wall, he was making hay. He certainly deserved his success, but it could just as easily have been mine.

### If your thinking is out of commission, you are generally out of a commission

I once made an appalling discovery. My office used the prospect registry system, whereby each salesman entered the name, address and phone number of each new prospect as he obtained one. At the end of a month, I counted the entries: there were over 100. Sales for the month totalled 25. What happened to the other 75? People obviously go into a real estate office to buy real estate.

There were many reasons why we didn't sell more of the 75 prospects, but one of the main ones, to my mind, was that personal emotions too often block the clear thinking of the real estate man.

When I set out to find the additional sales that would put me in the high income bracket, I remembered to think twice before anesthetizing my brain with grief and disappointment over the loss of one sale. Quite the opposite; at such a time it was particularly wise to be alert.

### Points to remember

1. When a house is sold, the seller often becomes a buyer.
2. In real estate, most sales first take place in the mind of the salesman.
3. Almost everything that happens in life opens the possibility for a sale of real estate, even the sale you missed.
4. You are out of business during the time spent in disappointment or anger.

# CHAPTER 17

# THE DAY I SOLD A LILAC BUSH FOR $30,000

When you begin selling footbridges, snowdrifts, or mountain views for thousands of dollars, you have reached a high plateau of selling that will bring you excitement, intense pleasure, and a very large income. This is the area that I call "the romance of selling real estate." I once sold a lilac bush for THIRTY THOUSAND DOLLARS. How it happened will be described shortly.

### The romance in selling real estate

There is the touch of the artist to selling in this manner. Most real estate people shy away from the romance of selling. This is indeed a shame, because it is the easiest method of selling there is, and tremendously rewarding. What feature causes a buyer to decide, at a given instant, that he wants to buy a certain house? Let's see how it's done.

1. Be ever alert to an unusual or unique feature of the homes listed for sale which sets them apart from the run-of-the-mill listings.
    a. These are features that other salesmen may overlook or ignore because they believe them to be liabilities.
2. Memorize indelibly the price and address of each of these properties, and their particular points of distinction. Many of the points to watch for are listed in Chapter 11.

3. During conversation with your prospects, a chance remark will often light the way for you to sell a pine tree or a fish pond. Frequently, these chance remarks fly through the air like a spark, and you will miss them if you are not alert. As an example, I once had a prospect who casually remarked that he owned a small plane. I just happened to know of a property that had its own landing strip. The home was not exactly the type he was looking for, but he bought it. Rather, he bought the landing strip, and the house went with it.

## HOME BUYERS GENERALLY BUY WITH THEIR HEARTS AND NOT THEIR HEADS

There is no denying that buyers today are quality conscious, but that doesn't necessarily have anything to do with what they will buy. Before they start house hunting, they are the recipients of much advice about what to look for in a well-built home, what to buy and what not to buy. They will make a list of requirements which they sincerely intend to follow during their search. All this they do with their heads. But when they first see *the* house, their pulses quicken, they get starry-eyed, and they fall in love with it. If it happens to be of good quality and, fortunately, it usually is, it's strictly a coincidence. Forgotten is all the advice, the long checklist: they buy the house with their hearts.

### Sentiment is salable

It is my confirmed belief that this phenomenon occurs in the majority of all residential sales. Often a special feature of a property, striking a sentimental chord in the buyer, will produce an almost instant sale. I trained my ear to listen for clues to these features, for they can be easily missed in casual conversation. The excitement of recognizing such clues made selling real estate the thrilling business it was and still is to me. Other than earning a $900 commission, what could be more thrilling than selling a lilac bush for $30,000? That's what happened in—

## THE STORY OF THE LILAC BUSH

Mr. and Mrs. Hornsby were returning to the midwest from a southwestern state. For three years, as Mrs. Hornsby said, she had seen nothing but endless miles of brown, baked earth, treeless and colorless, stretching to the horizon. She was a farm girl from Ohio and was delighted beyond words to be coming back to the rolling hills and green woods of the midwest.

They arrived at my office early in the morning, eager to look at homes. Mrs. Hornsby was like a child loose in a candy store: she didn't know which to grab first. In fact, that was the problem. Her enthusiasm for all of them, rather than any particular one, left me puzzled about which house to start closing. She was so taken with the green lawns, the trees, shrubbery and flower beds that she paid little attention to the features of the houses. Shortly after we left the last house on my list, however, Mrs. Hornsby gave me the winning clue when she said,

"Many times at night I've dreamed of being surrounded by lilac trees like those we had in Ohio. I could even smell the fragrance of them."

### A pre-selected home in my mental inventory became the target

Many homes in our area had lilac bushes growing around them, but one house listed with us had what must have been the champion of them all. It also had old-fashioned porches, railings, and lattice along the eaves, quite different from the modern home they said they preferred.

When we pulled up to the house, I told them there was something special I wanted them to see before we left. Mrs. Hornsby walked through the house slowly and quietly, and I thought I detected a reminiscent look on her face. After we inspected all of the rooms, we paused in the kitchen for a chat.

"How does this home appeal to you?" I asked.

Mr. Hornsby answered, "I think we'd still prefer a more modern home. We'd have to put built-ins in this kitchen, change light fixtures, and do further renovating that would make it pretty costly."

Mrs. Hornsby added, "Our furniture wouldn't fit in this style home. I do like it, but I think we'd better stay with a newer home."

### Proper timing is demonstrated by showing the house FIRST

"Okay," I said, "that's just what we'll do. By the way, I told you there was something special here I wanted you to see."

I opened the door leading to the rear yard, and stood aside for Mrs. Hornsby to go through. She took a half dozen steps and stopped. There in the exact center of the beautiful lawn stood a huge, perfectly shaped lilac tree. It was a veritable mountain of purple—a thing of beauty to behold. The air was heavy with lavender fragrance.

Mrs. Hornsby walked forward like a child approaching a Christmas tree. Suddenly she whirled about and cried to her husband,

"Jack, I love this place. Let's buy it."

And they did. That lilac tree cost Mr. Hornsby $30,000.

## UNIQUE FEATURES AND UNUSUAL CLUES THAT LED TO SALES

### The diamond ring

My sales manager passed this story on to me, and in my opinion it is a perfect example of recognizing, at the proper moment, a clue that produced a sale.

One busy Sunday afternoon a lady came to the office in answer to an ad on a home in the low-to-medium price class. Since all the salesmen were busy, the sales manager took her out. The prospect was very charming, very nicely dressed—white gloves and all. She was not at all pleased with the house described in the ad, so the sales manager showed her others in the same price class. However, she showed little interest in any of them, and they finally headed for the office. Along the way, the lady slipped off her gloves to light a cigarette, and on her middle finger was a ring with a diamond "that looked like the headlight on a locomotive," the sales manager said. She took one look at that "hunk of ice," turned at the next corner, and drove to a house that was more than twice the price of the house in the ad. It was an outstanding piece of property, well over the $30,000 mark, but it turned out to be precisely what the lady was looking for.

The sales manager had read the clue correctly. Her prospect had been giving in to a woman's infatuation with bargain-hunting. I learned a lesson from that.

## THE THREE-CAR FAMILY

An experience of mine paralleled that of the lady with the diamond ring in many ways. It started in mid-afternoon and ended at midnight. Snow had been falling most of the day, and the response to our weekend ads was below normal. About three o'clock, Mr. and Mrs. Petrok arrived with their family of six small children. They had sold their home in the city and, since Saturday was the only day they could both look, they were there ready to do business, snowstorm or no snowstorm. They were carrying the classified section of the newspaper, on which they had circled one of our ads. It was a two-story residence with almost an acre of land, priced at $17,500. I made the mistake of jumping to conclusions during the qualifying period. Because I didn't inquire further into Mr. Petrok's income and business position, I had the wrong picture entirely. This assumption almost lost me a sale.

**Jumping to conclusions leads you far afield.** When I took them to the house they had inquired about, they spent so long considering it that I thought it was a near-miss, and that if I continued to show them similar properties I would soon hit on the right one. We continued to look at homes for the rest of the afternoon. They discussed each one very seriously; how they could remodel it, improve on it, or add to it.

I assumed they had a modest income and were trying to buy a home that would both fit their family and fall within their means. How wrong I was! As long as I was willing to try to find them a large, expensive house in a low price bracket, they were willing to let me. I didn't realize this, but I knew something was wrong, so I decided to dig for clues by asking questions. I didn't have to dig very deeply—in fact, the clue leaped out at me with Mr. Petrok's very first answer.

Because all the children were along, I had been riding with him in his station wagon. Since we apparently had accomplished nothing in our house hunting, we were heading for the office.

**One question, and everything comes into focus.** "How do you like the station wagon?" I asked.

"I haven't driven it enough to really tell," he said. "I drive a Cadillac or sometimes my wife's Buick; we just have the wagon to knock around in."

Bingo! There it was! They were a THREE-CAR FAMILY—three expensive cars at that—and I had been showing them low-priced homes! My mind raced furiously, reviewing the houses that might interest this couple.

**Attracting ATTENTION, developing INTEREST, creating DESIRE, all in a couple of moments.** It was dark, it was snowing hard, and the children were hungry and restless. I felt sure I would have to hit the target dead center if I were to sell these people tonight. With another question or two I learned that Mr. Petrok owned his own business, a piece of information that I should have uncovered hours earlier. A few blocks from the office I asked him to pull over and stop for a moment.

"I know it's late, and I know you're tired, but there is a home that recently came on the market which is so unusual and so beautiful I wish you'd take a few minutes to look at it. It has four acres, a large, lovely house and a small barn, all enclosed with a white wooden fence. It's a perfect place for your family. This is the kind of property that is very hard to find. If you'll take the time to look at it, I know you will be glad you did."

"What's the price?" asked Mr. Petrok.

"It's well within your means, but let's look at it first," I answered. "We can be there in less than ten minutes."

He sat quietly for a moment, then turned the car around and we were on our way. We stopped once so that I could call the owner and have him turn on all the lights in the house and the floodlights outside. When we pulled into the lighted, snow-covered driveway, the scene was as pretty as a Christmas card. The thirty-foot living room with a roaring fire in the fireplace won the hearts of my buyers. Mrs. Petrok liked everything about the house, particularly the large, farm-style kitchen.

**Observing the property selling itself.** Finally Mr. Petrok and I went outside, for he decided to look over the entire property. By now the snow had turned to sleet, and there was a thin crust of ice on top of a foot of snow: nevertheless, Mr. Petrok, armed with a flashlight, walked every inch of the boundaries of the four acres, and I tagged along. With every step I broke through the ice crust and shoved more snow up my pants leg. I was cold, wet, and exhausted, but I was selling real estate. We finally made it back to the house, and before we went inside Mr. Petrok asked the price of the property again.

It was $40,000. For the next two hours the Petroks and the Pattons, who owned the property, talked about it. I held my breath for fear the subject of the price would come up, but it didn't. If my buyers wanted to make an offer, I wanted them to make it to me, not to the Pattons.

At about eleven o'clock we took our leave, and I felt a sale in the making. After Mr. Petrok spent ten minutes scraping ice off the windshield, we headed for the office, with the children all asleep in the back of the car. My prospect and his wife chatted excidedly about the property. I knew Mr. Patton was very firm on his price, so when Mr. Petrok asked me if I thought it could be bought for less, I answered,

"I don't think there's a chance."

By this time it was snowing again, and we were making headway very slowly, with Mr. Petrok lost in deep thought. Just as we pulled up at the office, he stated,

"I would be willing to pay $39,000."

**A verbal agreement to sign a written one.** I answered after a pause. "Mr. Petrok, I have a very strict rule never to take a verbal offer: however, under the circumstances, if you will come into the office with me, I'll call Mr. Patton and ask him if he'll accept your offer providing that, *if he does,* you will sign the purchase agreement *tonight.*"

He agreed, and I placed the call. Mr. Patton's response was,

"If he really means business, I'll take the $39,000."

While Mr. Petrok paced the floor and the snow piled deeper outside, I typed the purchase agreement. It was midnight when a very tired Mr. and Mrs. Petrok put their signatures on the contract. Then they piled into one of their three cars and headed home. I took my briefcase and wet feet and did the same.

## WATCH FOR AMENITIES THAT ARE MORE SALABLE THAN THE HOUSE ITSELF

At the foot of the hill on Blaine Place was a cottage that had been remodelled into a delightful little home. With new light fixtures, a modernized kitchen, light gold carpeting and freshly painted walls, it was enough to steal the heart of any woman. After all the time and money that the owners had spent, it was ironic that my buyers made little more than a cursory inspection of the home.

The side yard was spacious, and toward the rear of it stood the broadest tree I have ever seen. It was like a gigantic umbrella covered with dense green foliage. Starting seven or eight feet up from the ground, the branches grew straight out from the trunk for dozens of feet, in all directions. The tree stole the show.

My buyers had brought their three sons and an assortment of in-laws to help them house hunt. They looked through the house, then seemed to dismiss it as they stared with wonder and amazement at the grandeur of the tree. In a twinkling, the boys were lost among the branches, and the husband, who seemed knowledgeable, talked at great length with his in-laws about the possible age of the tree, the length and depth of its roots, and so forth. He'd never seen anything like it in his life, he said. He walked around and under it, stood back to admire it, and I am as sure as I can be that he bought the house to get the tree.

## A STAINED GLASS WINDOW RECALLS
## A SYMBOL OF SECURITY

"Charm" is a word usually reserved for describing older homes. It brings to mind winding stairs, french doors, archways, stained glass windows, and marble, and buyers of older homes always look for these amenities. However, I had the strange experience one time of selling a house to a lady simply because of a *single* stained glass window.

She had come into the office looking for a two-family home so that she could live in one part and rent the other. This type of property was very popular, and therefore commanded fairly high prices. I could find nothing to fit the lady's means, so I suggested a large residence near the high school, with the thought that she could rent rooms to teachers. The idea did not particularly appeal to her, but she agreed to look.

I felt I was losing ground from the time we entered the front door. She just wasn't in tune with the whole idea, and her interest was practically nil as we went from room to room. She was determined to stick with her original plan, and expressed disappointment that I couldn't produce what she wanted at a price she could afford.

**The motives were reversed; her comfort should come first.** After our first inspection I invited her to look again at the rooms which would be her living quarters. I wanted her to see the house as a home, and not as income property. We started the second inspection. She admired the china closet in the dining room, the large entry hall and open staircase, and the milk glass globes on the electric fixtures. The living room, which in this style house is more properly the parlor, was almost square, and had very high ceilings and a large bay window.

It was in this room that we paused to rest for a few moments. The lady seated herself and seemed lost in thought. I was quiet, deciding to let silence do the selling.

**Without silence, the effect of the stained glass window would have been lost.** Outside, the sun suddenly broke through the clouds and, as it did, there appeared across the lap of my prospect a multitude of small, multicolored squares. In fact, for a couple of feet on each side of her there were little blocks of red, yellow, blue and green, for across the top of the bay window were curved sections of mosaic stained glass. The occurrence caught my client by surprise and, as I watched her, there was no question but that some particular emotional reaction was taking place.

A few minutes passed before she arose to leave, and she was silent until we were seated in the car. Then she said,

"I'm going to buy that house, but would it be all right if I brought my brother to see it in the morning?"

It would be perfectly all right, I assured her. I was about to say goodbye to her at the office when she asked,

"Don't I have to sign some papers or something to buy the house?"

"I understood you were going to have your brother look at it first."

"That has nothing to do with buying the house," she said. "I have another reason for wanting him to see it."

**A story strange but true: why one prospect decided to buy.** After the sales contract had been drafted and she had signed it, I asked why she had decided to buy a house in which, at first, she had shown only slight interest.

"You'll think I'm a little crazy when I tell you," she replied.

This was her story. Her parents had been very poor, and her father was in ill health all during her childhood. They had moved from one rental house to another: each one, she said, in worse condition than the one before. Shortly after her tenth birthday she lost both parents within a few months. She and her younger brother then went to live with an aunt and stayed with her until they finished college.

Those were wonderful years, she declared. Her aunt had treated her well, and she had fond memories of the large old home where she had many happy times. But what she remembered the most was the room that was all her own. It also had a window containing a section of stained glass. She described how she had watched the pattern of color cast by the stained glass window move across the floor as she lay on her bed reading, studying, or just day-dreaming.

"I've been in a state of turmoil," she said, "about this house hunting, and this afternoon, almost as if it were meant to be, the security, happiness, and peace of mind of my childhood were brought back to me by the colors from the window of the house we just left. All at once I had a strong desire to own it, and that, believe it or not, is what made me decide to buy."

It *was* hard to believe, but more fun than not to.

**Fresh fallen snow turns the drab and ugly into scenes of beauty**

Mr. Smalley owned a house on Washington Street. He wanted very much to sell it, but for a while it looked as if he might have to give it away. It was well constructed, and he had dropped the price well below replacement cost, but there were some problems.

In the first place, the exterior of the house itself was very plain. It had all the appeal of a barn, and I could think of no way to correct it. Secondly, on each side there was a vacant lot and the house sat there like a stump in a field. Mr. Smalley had enclosed his property with a wooden fence and put a couple of spruce trees in front and some fruit trees along the drive, but the weed-grown, trash-covered lots next door, coupled with the plainness of the house, added to zero sales appeal.

**An unattractive home must somehow be made appealing.** He put the house on the market early in June. Throughout the summer months and into the fall it was shown a number of times because of the high quality-low price factor, but nobody wanted to buy the ugly duckling. Fall came and went, and other homes sold, but there was not a nibble on Mr. Smalley's home at any price.

Fortunately, Mr. Smalley was an amiable man, blessed with patience, and he was very appreciative of our efforts to sell his home. I remember saying to him,

"There's a buyer for every house, and one of these days one will come along for yours."

**A snowstorm did the job.** Winter was upon us and I reasoned that Mr. Smalley would have his house until spring. I reasoned wrong. An early winter snowstorm and an opportune phone call changed everything.

The snow started to fall on Saturday night a little after dark. It snowed all night long, and by morning over a foot had accumulated. The fresh whiteness turned the entire countryside into a winter wonderland.

Most of the phone calls to the office that Sunday morning were to cancel appointments made the day before, because of the storm, but one was an inquiry for property. The lady identified herself as Mrs. Neely and gave me an address on Elm Street. "We have old friends visiting with us over the weekend, and they are looking for a house. We do many things together, and we'd like to have them live close to us. Do you have any homes under $20,000 in our neighborhood?"

There was only one that I could think of. Mr. Smalley's house was a block over and a half block down. I gave Mrs. Neely a few details. She relayed the information to her friends, who wanted to see the home right away. I picked them up a few minutes later.

**Only the smoke from the chimney seemed real.** When we stopped in front of Mr. Smalley's home, I couldn't believe my eyes. The snow had covered all of the ugliness and transformed the house and grounds into a scene of unbelievable beauty. The two lots looked for all the world like white icing on top of a cake. The trees, fence and house had become a scene out of Whittier's "Snow-Bound."

The interior of the house had always been delightful, and with the price so reasonable, the house that wouldn't sell, sold easily. The following year houses were built on the adjoining lots, and the entire picture was different, but the fact remains that a snowstorm changed the ugly duckling into a white swan long enough for it to get a new owner.

**The golden bath I thought was elegant
made my prospect shudder**

In selling real estate it is very, very easy to say the wrong thing. It took me a while to learn to let the house sell itself. This is the story of a time I talked too much.

Mr. and Mrs. Bradley were seeking a *new* home, and were moving into our area from a neighboring state. They were very pleasant people, and discriminating buyers. They could afford an expensive home and were explicit about what they wanted. It had to be new, all on one floor, of brick construction, and with all the refinements of a luxury home.

We were handling new homes for some of the better builders in the area. I showed the Bradleys a number of these, but concentrated on one in particular which I thought was an outstandingly beautiful residence. There was an extra-long living room with red oak hardwood flooring, a coved ceiling, and a crab orchard stone fireplace. A large, formal dining room was fitted with wainscoting, a crystal chandelier, and a picture window. The fruitwood cabinets and built-ins in the large kitchen made it the answer to any woman's dreams. There were three spacious bedrooms and a panelled family room in the basement.

**A regal bathroom—it would have been better placed in a palace.** The builder had outdone himself, I thought, with the positively elegant bathroom off the master bedroom. The cabinets were white, trimmed with gold. Above the marble counter top was a wall-to-wall plate glass mirror. The faucet turns were shaped like roses, and gold-plated. The floor was white vinyl tile, with flecks of gold. The entire bathroom glistened and sparkled, even more since all four walls were covered with gold-colored ceramic tile. I had never seen such an elegant bathroom.

I could hardly wait for Mrs. Bradley to see the rest of the house so that I could show her this golden bathroom. She admitted the house had everything they wanted.

When there were no wild exclamations over the bath, I chalked it up to the fact that its dazzling beauty had struck her speechless. Quite unnecessarily, I recounted each item, from the gold faucets to the marble tops, and expressed my opinion that it was positively the most fabulous bathroom I had ever seen—it was doubtful that a king's palace had its equal. It must have seemed that I was trying to sell her a bathroom instead of a house.

My confidence was a little shaken when I couldn't get them to agree to buy the house, but they did consent to return the following day for another inspection. We retraced our steps the next day, ending at the home with my gorgeous bath. All the lights were ablaze, and it sparkled like a jewel. Mrs. Bradley examined the house again, as well as the master bath, and, as I watched her, I sensed that this was the right house. But for all my efforts they would not agree to buy it.

**I was the hang-up, but I didn't know it.** The third day the Bradleys were still without a home. I decided it was time for the shakedown technique, so we got down to the facts of the matter.

"Unless my salesman's intuition is completely out of order, I know the house you people are interested in, but for some reason you are hesitant about buying it. It's the one with the elegant bathroom. Tell me, what's the problem? It's the house you like the most—why don't you buy it?"

They glanced at each other; then Mrs. Bradley said,

"I haven't had the heart to tell you, but I can't stand that gilded bathroom. In the first place, it looks like something out of Hollywood, and I don't go for that. The real problem, though, is those yellow walls. When I stood before the mirror it turned my complexion a light green. I simply couldn't live with that bath. That's the reason we haven't bought the house."

If I had kept my mouth shut, she would have told me all of this the first day. I had wasted enough time talking too much. We drove to the builder's office and I assured him we had a sale if he would make certain alterations. He had to agree to change the tile, take out the gold faucets, and tone down the golden bathroom in general.

He did so, reluctantly but wisely, and the sale was made. That was how I learned that the theory "Silence is Golden" sells better than a golden bathroom.

### Points to remember

1. Home buyers generally buy with their hearts and not with their heads.

2. Watch for amenities that are more salable than the house itself.
3. Often, if you miss the clue, you miss the sale.
4. Not to speak, is to speak volumes when showing a home.
5. Because you think a certain feature is great doesn't mean everyone will.

CHAPTER **18**

# HOW I TURNED A COMPETITOR'S MISTAKE INTO A QUICK SALE

It would appear to be a rare occasion to have some-one you don't know hand you a check for hundreds of dollars. In the real estate business it happens more often than you would believe. It happens because somewhere a competitor, dealing with a prospect, made a mistake. If you are alert, and looking for the occasional additional sales, you can be the recipient of these ricochet prospects. You will be pleasantly surprised at what happens if you form the habit of asking new clients each and every time, during the qualifying period,

"Have you been shown property by any other realty office?"

### The jackpot question: why didn't they buy it?

If the answer is yes, then dig in! Try to find out what homes they have seen, and if they felt the other real estate man understood their needs and desires. Most important, discover whether or not they saw any homes that they particularly liked.

If the other office did make a mistake, here's where you will find it out, and very possibly you can cash in on the situation. If they had been shown a home they liked very much, then ask them why they didn't buy it.

Listen carefully to their answer, for it may be worth hundreds and sometimes thousands of dollars to you.

A prospect's answer, consisting of *four words,* once earned me a

183

very quick ONE THOUSAND THREE HUNDRED AND FIFTY DOLLARS! He had been shown a home he really liked by a salesman from another office.

"Why didn't you buy it?" I inquired.

"HE DIDN'T ASK ME!" was the astonishing answer.

### The good fortune of getting
### a prospect on the rebound

When prospects who aren't "seasoned" buyers, so to speak, walk into an office, the salesman involved sets about to educate them, which is proper and professional. Most prospects distrust all salesmen to some degree and don't immediately accept everything they are told. Although the salesman is probably doing an excellent job, enough resentment toward the educational process creeps into the prospect's mind to prevent him from doing business with this particular real estate man. During this time the prospect has also been shown a number of homes, and he has therefore become somewhat aware of market values. Later, when prospects such as these came into my office, I was in for a fairly easy sale. Someone else had done the preliminary work.

It was an entirely different matter, however, when a competitor made an outright mistake that resulted in an immediate and effortless sale for me. All I needed was awareness.

### My competitor made the sale,
### and I made the commission

This is a story where the ending must be told before the beginning.

Mr. Kelly had stopped in the office after work to tell me the type of house he and his wife were looking for, and to make an appointment with me for the following day to see some homes. During the qualifying period I asked if they had already seen many houses.

"Yes, we've seen quite a few."

"Was there any one that you liked particularly well?"

"One house," he replied, "we liked very much."

"Tell me about it," I said, "maybe I have something similar to it."

"I can do better than that," he said. "I can show it to you. It's not far from here."

"Fine. Let's go."

### "He didn't ask me"

On the way to the house he told me that a real estate man from another office had shown them this property the previous weekend. He then began to sell the house to me. With considerable enthusiasm he told me all the features of the house that he liked. He even leaned forward to get a look at the house while we were still a half block away. My thought was, this certainly is *the* house for this man. I didn't know why he hadn't bought it, but I was going to find out. We sat in the driveway for a little while; then I asked Mr. Kelly to excuse me for a couple of moments. I went to the front door and talked briefly with the owner. When I returned I had all the pertinent facts I needed to know about the property, including the price and the owner's name, and his permission to sell.

I said to Mr. Kelly, "This is indeed an outstanding home. Would you like to buy it?"

"Yes," he answered, "I would."

We made a beeline for the office.

From the material I had scribbled on the back of an envelope, we drew up a sales agreement which Mr. Kelly signed. He also gave me a check for an earnest money deposit. But I still had to know the answer to the big question.

"Tell me something," I said. "When the other real estate man showed you the house last week, why didn't you buy it from him?"

"He didn't ask me," was his reply.

Puzzling? Indeed.

Did Mr. Kelly wonder how I could list the house and sell it to him so quickly? I don't know. He didn't ask me.

### The calculated referral that boomeranged

One blustery March day a tall, elderly Ichabod Crane walked in the office and asked for me. He wore steel-rimmed glasses and a battered old hat; his suit went back a couple of generations, and he had the blackened nails and scarred hands of a workingman. When he introduced himself as Mr. Fisher, he was so soft-spoken I could barely hear him. He explained that he was looking for run-down property that he could fix up to rent. He wanted to buy in the $7,500 to $8,000 range. He added that he had just come from a real estate office down the street where they had told him that they didn't have what he wanted, but that I specialized in this sort of property and was the person to see.

Such property as Mr. Fisher was looking for was almost non-existent in our area: even if there were any, the commission involved was so small it hardly paid to handle it. One of my friendly competitors had decided to have a little fun.

**My competitor was joking but the prospect was serious.** When I realized what they'd done I decided to try to have a little fun of my own. Thinking perhaps there was more here than first appeared, I decided to look under the surface, which my competitor had failed to do. I learned that Mr. Fisher already owned a number of properties which he had renovated, that he had cash on hand, and that he didn't care about the condition of the houses when he bought them. If they were priced right, he would buy. I had to find some property for Mr. Fisher somehow, if I were going to have my share of the fun.

**One big sale or half a dozen little ones is all the same.** After giving it a little thought, I remembered a builder who took houses in trade. I gave him a call, and luck was with me. He had taken in a small house which was indeed run down, and he would be tickled to death to get it off his hands at a price of $8,000. He gave me the address, and told me the key was in the mailbox. I relayed all this to Mr. Fisher and he decided to go to look at it. In a short time he was back and in a soft, almost apologetic voice he said, "I will pay $7,000 for it."

I called the builder and gave him this information.

"Tell the man he's bought a house," he replied.

Mr. Fisher fixed up the house and quickly rented it to a young couple. He became a fairly regular visitor to the office and, as time went by, I sold him a number of properties in the same manner.

I always hoped my friendly competitor got a good laugh because that's all he got. The commission was mine: a small one, true, but spendable.

### A competitor who gave up too easily

I suspect the mistake of giving up too easily is made quite often by people selling real estate. When this occurs, someone loses and someone wins. If you are an enterprising person with just a touch of audacity you can be the winner. In one instance in my million dollar year I made a sale amounting to $21,500 because one of my competitors gave up too easily.

A man and his wife stopped by our office on a Sunday afternoon looking for a particular type of home they wanted to buy. During the qualifying period I asked them if they had been house hunting long, and then came the now-standard key question:

"Have you seen any homes you liked particularly well?"

"Yes," they said, "as a matter of fact we have. Yesterday a gentleman from another office showed us a home that we liked exceptionally well from the outside. However, we weren't able to see the inside because the owners are out of town over the weekend."

When they told me the address I recognized the home as belonging to the Smiths. They had given permission to show the house when they were away, and arranged to leave a key in the garage so that the house could be shown at any time. Apparently they had gone on a weekend trip and inadvertently neglected to leave the key. My prospects said they intended to look at the house the following day with my competitor, but in the meantime had decided to keep looking at other houses.

"If a salesman from some other office locates a relative who has a key, or runs down the whereabouts of the Smiths, the house may be sold before you have a chance to look at it tomorrow," I told them.

"I hope not!" the wife said, with much concern. "I think that house is just what we've been looking for."

"Would you like to see the interior right now if I could arrange it?"

The husband answered, "We would indeed."

When we arrived at the home, the owners were still away and the key was still missing from its hiding place. The expression of admiration on the faces of my prospects as they walked around the property prompted me to say,

"If you like the inside of this house as well as you do the outside, are you ready to buy it?"

The husband answered, "I believe we are."

I decided it was time to be a little brazen and, since I knew the Smith family well, I had but small qualms about my plan. I took my flashlight from the car, walked to the door of the back porch, knocked out a small pane of glass, and reached in and unlocked the door.

We made the inspection and I won my gamble, for they bought the house. Replacing the glass cost me seventy-nine cents, and a dime's worth of putty. The commission on the sale was $1,290.

A very important aftermath was that the Smiths told me later they had found a note, put under the door by still a third real estate office, asking them to call if they got home Sunday night, regardless of the hour. This office had buyers who needed only to inspect the interior to make their decision. I've always felt that I probably saved this home for my prospects, who wanted it very much, by breaking a small pane of glass.

I don't go around breaking out people's windows, but in this isolated case it seemed worth the risk. The point of the story, of course, is, don't give up too easily. There is a solution to every problem if you will think your way through.

### Points to remember

1. When you get a prospect on the rebound, most of your work has already been done.
2. Many people won't tell you they want to buy a certain house unless you ask them.
3. Don't pre-judge a prospect. He may have an untidy appearance, but a neat bank account.

# CHAPTER 19

# THREE OVERLOOKED SOURCES
# FOR EASY SALES

I'd venture to say that on your way to work this morning you drove by thousands of dollars which are just waiting to be picked up. These dollars are represented by various types of residential and business buildings whose best usage and highest value have been downgraded by obsolescence, ravages of time, and changes in zoning. They literally cry out for listing and handling by a knowledgeable, creative real estate man. They often represent tremendous profits to a developer, improvements in appearance as as well as additional tax revenue to the city, and large commissions to YOU.

### Three main sources of overlooked listings

1. Dilapidated homes that require renovating or are on land which can easily be rezoned for business or industrial purposes.
2. Older business buildings occupying land sufficiently valuable to justify construction of a new business building.
3. Lots or acreage lying on the periphery of an expanding community.

If you are sincerely interested in earning THIRTY TO FORTY THOUSAND DOLLARS A YEAR, don't expect it to fall in your lap. You must be a little creative. If you believe that developing the kind of sales described above is complicated and difficult, you are mistaken. It is a type of selling which is exciting, easy, and very profitable. Let's take a look at how it's done.

## THE NEGLECTED RESIDENCE

In your city, as well as in mine, there are any number of older homes, often vacant, obviously in need of attention, that are a liability both to the owner and to the community. There are reasons why these properties are in their present condition.

Our first step is to learn the story behind these neglected homes. Often a visit to one or more of the neighbors will give you that story, as well as the name and address of the owner. If not, a trip to the county assessor's office will reveal who is paying the taxes on the property. Once you've located the owner, the battle is half won, and you're on your way to a nice commission. Other real estate people will drive by this property daily and say to themselves, There's a home I could do something with—I wonder who owns it. You have a tremendous advantage because you now *know* who owns it.

### Renovate and price high
### versus as is and price low

The next step is a discussion with the owner. It is fairly certain that he will be interested in professional help and advice on how to get his money out of the property. He will be impressed and pleased to know that you are interested in helping him. The main question will be: is he able and willing to renovate the property and thus sell it at its highest value, or is it to his best interest to sell it as is at a price low enough to allow the purchaser to bear the cost of renovation and still leave a margin of profit?

To establish a selling price, whichever course is chosen, it is necessary for you to determine the cost of remodeling. Ask the owner to obtain bids from two or possibly three contractors, and also to get an estimate on putting the grounds in top shape. While this is being done, there's no reason why you can't begin your search for a buyer. Contact the people on your list who specialize in buying, renovating, and reselling older homes. If you don't have such a list, start one *now*. There are literally fortunes to be made buying rundown property, renovating it, and reselling it, and many people spend all their time doing just that—find out who they are in your area.

### Newspaper ad headings aimed at investors

An excellent way to find buyers for this type of property is through newspaper ads. Prospects for such deals search the ads daily. Here are some headlines I have used effectively:

OLDER HOME NEEDS REMODELING
HANDYMAN'S SPECIAL
LITTLE WORK LARGE PROFIT
SPECULATOR'S DREAM
FIX UP CASH IN
DIAMOND IN THE ROUGH
SACRIFICING OLDER HOME
LOW PRICE HIGH POTENTIAL

A For Sale sign on the property will bring a lot of calls. In any event, I assure you you will have no difficulty in locating interested prospects.

## THE PERCENTAGE OF PROFIT IS THE REGULATING FACTOR

The technique for selling speculation property is vastly different from that for selling a house which is to become the residence of the purchaser. You are now dealing strictly with the profit factor. Your prospect will probably be a man thoroughly experienced with remodeling costs. He is used to high profits. You can do all the selling you want to, but unless the percentage of profit is there, it will be in vain.

Your buyer will take the price you have quoted him, add the cost of remodeling, the real estate commission, title costs, and other expenses he will have on resale. He will also add taxes, interest on his money, and upkeep during the time necessary to resell it; a reasonable time period would not exceed six months. He will then subtract that total from what he believes the remodeled house will bring. If that amount which represents his profit interests him, you have a sale. If it is too low, he will make an offer. If that is refused, he will walk away.

### The seller must leave some profit
### for the investor

About the only problem that arises in sales of this kind is that the owners usually want most of the profit for themselves. They are not willing to sell at a price low enough to permit a resale profit. Therefore, at the time you take the listing, and after determining all the costs involved, you have to convince the seller that he must leave a profit sufficient to interest a developer for his work, time, investment, knowledge and risk.

If you do this, you will never have an easier sale. In fact, you will have a double sale if you handle it right, because the story is not ended until a profit has been generated by the resale of the remodeled home.

### The double sale

Once you've consummated your sale with the speculator, it is certainly worth your effort to solicit the listing of the property when the remodeling is finished. There's usually a reluctance on the part of the speculator to cooperate, because your commission cuts deeply into his profit, but I found I could generally overcome this by being as helpful as possible. I could do some of the legwork, telephone to contact the various tradesmen, locate materials, and have the house open when necessary. The persuasive point in getting the listing, however, was that I could sell the property quickly, and this time factor would produce a savings to the speculator in the form of interest, taxes, and maintenance. Also, his invested dollars, as well as his profit, would be released, which enabled him to move on to the next project. In the field of real estate speculation a quick turnover is essential for a good annual profit percentage.

## SHARP APPRECIATION OFTEN MAKES
## PROPERTY TOO VALUABLE TO USE
## AS A RESIDENCE

Another type of double sale arises when the subject property is occupied by the owner. Usually the owners are willing to sell only because something has come about to cause a sharp increase in the value of their property. Appreciation results from:

1. Rezoning of a street or area.
2. Annexation.
3. The property lying in the path of an expanding community.
4. A demand for homesites appreciating the value of the land, percentage-wise, more than that of the residence.

### Tie the first sale into the second one

To work this type of property you must determine that, in fact, one of the above conditions exists. Assure the owners that you will work diligently to obtain the highest dollar for their house that can be reasonably expected from a prudent buyer on the open market.

You can practically clinch a double sale by guaranteeing them that in the terms of the sales agreement you will allow sufficient time before they must surrender possession of the property for YOU to locate THEM another house to buy. Anticipate their questions, and have the answers. Know what is to be done, tell them, and do it. You'll have a double commission, and if it happens that you sell to a speculator, you may even have a triple one.

## THE DISSOLVING ACRES

A drive to the outskirts of your city on a scheduled once-a-week basis should unquestionably become a part of your real estate career. This practice will keep you current with the economic direction of your area, and it will frequently uncover an opportunity to earn a nice commission and, occasionally, a staggering one. Farms, ranches, and dormant parcels of land, once far out and sometimes almost inaccessible, become regional shopping centers, golf courses, or subdivisions, seemingly overnight. Then the next adjacent strip of quiet land becomes susceptible to society's need for more room to live, and the entire process is repeated. Millions of dollars are expended by developers, and the involvement of real estate men is indispensable.

You should be one of those involved! You will like the increase in your income. The next time you're out for a drive in the country, and you are surprised to come upon this new subdivision, or you wonder when they started that shopping center, remember: you are seeing developments that lined some real estate man's pockets with gold. Why couldn't it have been you?

## THE CONVERSION OF A
## NEGLECTED RESIDENCE

One of my experiences with a "cold turkey" listing involved an old, weatherbeaten, two-story, frame residence that I had driven past probably hundreds of times. One day I had my eyes open as well as my mind, and as I approached the house it was apparent that construction of business buildings was closing in on the old place. On impulse I stopped and rang the doorbell, and asked the owner if he were interested in selling the property.

"Not particularly," was his answer.

However, he hastily added that if he *were* to sell he would have to get $17,000. He acted as if he were half-ashamed to ask this price for a home in such poor condition. I told him I'd like to list it, and would see what I could do to get his asking price.

### A $10,000 house brings $17,000

I knew I'd hit the jackpot, because his house was located on the corner of two busy thoroughfares. By the next morning I had a signed purchase contract on his house for $17,000. A few months later I resold it for $39,000, and shortly after that a beautiful, brick business building occupied the site. I admired that building every time I saw it as if it were partly mine. One thing more: I sold the original owner a duplex for $21,000, making a total of $77,000 in sales to be part of my million dollar year, and generating a commission of $4,620. All because I rang a doorbell!

## THE BUILDING THAT SOLD FOR
## A MINUS $5,000

The Waldo building had been sitting in the 2100 block for so long that it was overlooked and forgotten, like an old dent in the rear fender. A restaurant chain wishing to build in our city had half the local real estate men, including me, searching for a location. We were all hunting furiously for a lot to fill their needs.

Suddenly, I knew where there was one. It was under the Waldo building. A call to the owner confirmed that he would sell—at his price, of course. Negotiations were started, and my buyers liked the location, but they rejected his price of $50,000. They would pay that much if the lot were vacant but, because they estimated demolition costs to run at least $5,000, they were willing to pay only $45,000. We eventually made the deal at that figure.

The building sold for $5,000 less than nothing, but the land earned a commission of $2,700.


## HOW TO CREATE A LIFETIME PROSPECT

Real estate people are forever being approached by friends or acquaintances who say, "If you ever run across something hot that I can make a nice profit on, give me a call."

In my opinion, 99 percent of these well-intentioned, would-be speculators are a lost cause. The 1 percent, however, can make up for the others. They all, no doubt, have the money, but only 1 percent has the guts.

### The proof is in the profit and, once made, you are in control

If you're lucky enough to pick one of the 1 percent, you have a lifetime prospect. After you've made the first profitable deal for him, he's your pawn. He will buy and sell when and in whatever manner you advise. It is a mutual money-making combination. Acquire a half dozen of his kind, with money and courage to speculate, add this to your regular business, and you're on easy street.

### A would-be speculator's moment of truth

At luncheon one day Dick had given me that old 'if you ever run across' business, and I mentally filed him away to test him on some future date. Some months later I had ferreted out a land investment opportunity that, if one didn't know the facts, looked like a big nothing. I knew the facts, however. It was HOT property! As part of my plan, I purposely called Dick very, very early in the morning. I wouldn't allow him time even for breakfast.

"You wanted to be a speculator in real estate, you said, so let's go."

Thirty minutes later, I turned into a narrow gravel road, drove about two miles, then stopped by a field that was half swamp and half hills.

"There you are, Dick," I said. "Thirty acres for $70,000, which will start you on your way to being a rich man."

The expression on his face left no doubt that he thought I was crazy, and he pointedly told me so. I timed a dramatic pause perfectly, then started the car. Before we left, I had a little "educating" to do.

### Establishing your position firmly
### for present and future deals

"Dick," I said, "I want to tell you something. You don't have to buy this land, but I resent your insinuation that I would offer you an investment proposition that wasn't a good risk. If you lack the courage to be a speculator, there's nothing I can do about it.

"You're a dentist, and I wouldn't think of telling you how to pull a tooth. I'm in the real estate business, and from a speculation standpoint you are in no way qualified to tell me that a piece of land is a good investment or not. If we're going to work as a team and create a profit, then I'll do the finding and you do the buying.

"One of the richest men in America has publicly stated over and over again that he acquired a great portion of his wealth by associating himself with real estate men in various sections of the country, then doing what they told him without question."

### Don't de-escalate your position
### by revealing the results of your research

Dick looked at the swamp again, and said,
"You must know something I don't."
"It's my business to know."
"George," he said, "I'm confident you know your business. I'll buy it if you say so."

I replied, "Buy it!" and he did.

The little gravel road soon became a four-lane, paved thorough-fare. Less than a mile to the east, construction started on a shopping center that was to be one of the largest in the world. A neighboring suburb, interested in the revenue, annexed the shopping center site. Dick's 30 acres lay in between. A direct line for the sewer and water pipes ran along the south boundary of the property. The suburb needed an easement: we needed high-rise zoning. Both needs were granted, but there was one stipulation. Only 60 percent of the land could be built on.

There were to be 260 apartment units allowed. Dick did not have the time, money, or knowledge to develop the project, but he found a developer who did. The price for the newly zoned land was $1,000 a unit—$260,000 for a $70,000 investment! The plans called for four separate apartment buildings, each one on its own hilltop.

## LEARN TO SELL ON PURPOSE, NOT BY ACCIDENT

Things don't just happen: someone makes them happen. The next time you pass an older, rundown residence, an outdated business building, or vacant land just beyond the city limits, stop—and MAKE something happen.

If I could only persuade you to try it, just once, the success you would experience would soon have you searching for such properties. The best persuader I can think of is to point out that you would add thousands of dollars to your income. As I understand it, the main purpose of the real estate business is to sell real estate. These properties we have been discussing represent real estate *waiting* to be sold, so, by thunder, let's sell it!

### Points to remember

1. Creative selling is:
   a. Locating property that needs to be sold.
   b. Selling your idea to the seller, then
   c. Selling the property to a buyer.

2. Develop a list of the names of people who buy property to renovate and resell.
3. Don't stop with the first sale; the seller either needs another home or has capital released that should be reinvested. Always aim for the double sale.
4. The real estate man with an average income handles only the business that comes to him. Those in the high-income bracket go out and create it.

# CHAPTER 20

# SHORT-TERM EXCLUSIVES THAT BROUGHT ME EXTRA SALES

It is foolish to list a house exclusively for only one day, right? WRONG! If a 24-hour exclusive is the best you can get, TAKE IT! You will speed up your selling processes and hone a sharp edge on your salesmanship. You might even sell the property! It only takes ONE day to sell a house—why not the FIRST day?

### Pressure produces sales

Working under pressure commands action. The shorter the time, the harder you'll work. You are literally FORCED to sell. You'll get some of those additional sales we are after if you are willing to take the exclusive for whatever length of time you can get: two weeks, one week, over a weekend, or even ONE DAY. More than once I have listed a home exclusively for 90 days and had it sell the FIRST day. In one instance, only three hours passed between the signing of the exclusive and the signing of the sales agreement. If I am free to do so, I will take an exclusive listing for whatever period of time I can persuade the owner to agree to, be it one month or one day!

### Hard work for a short time
### encourages an extended exclusive

Another advantage of the short-term exclusive is that it gives you the opportunity to show the owner that you are industrious and are trying hard to sell his home. Once he is convinced of this, he may possibly agree to an extension of a much longer period.

It should be pointed out that the value of a short-term exclusive applies only to properties with a fairly high degree of salability. It would be nonsensical to attempt it with anything less.

## THE FOLLY OF
## "90 DAYS OR ELSE" EXCLUSIVES

Real estate people employed in offices that are members of a Multiple Listing Service are, of course, regulated by these services, whose rules discourage, if not prohibit, exclusive listings for less than 90 days. There are good and understandable reasons why this must be: the high cost of processing, for one thing, prohibits short exclusives. Independent real estate offices, however, are in a more advantageous position, and with no great risk or cost, they do not need to establish a minimum time limit since everything is handled in one office.

### The commission on the sale of a short exclusive
### is the same as on a long one

Speaking from my experiences, I would like to suggest to the brokers and sales people of independent offices that they experiment with short-term exclusives where long-term exclusives are not possible. After all, the sale is the thing, and a little time exclusively is better than none at all. To my way of thinking, when a seller cannot be convinced to grant a 90-day exclusive, for a real estate man to demand it "or else" is utter foolishness. This attitude will lose him and his office many, many dollars in commissions. Let us compare the two.

### An exclusive is an agreement
### among three parties, not two

The processing of a 90-day exclusive is a sort of three-way partnership among the owner, the salesman, and the salesman's office.

1. THE OWNER'S RESPONSIBILITIES:
   a. To allow his home to be priced to the market.
   b. To put the interior and exterior of his home in top condition, and keep it that way.
   c. To make the property accessible for showings at all reasonable hours.
   d. To refrain from interfering in any way with the salesman and his prospect.

2. THE SALESMAN'S RESPONSIBILITIES:
   a. To advise the owner authoritatively on price, and how to prepare his home for market.
   b. To make a record of the pertinent details of the property, so as to be able to discuss it with a prospect accurately and intelligently.
   c. To arrange for inspection by his co-workers.
   d. To expose the property through signs, newspaper ads, and word of mouth.
   e. To service the listing by notifying the owners of newspaper ads planned, holding Open House on the property, and phoning in advance, when possible, of intended showings.
   f. To work diligently to get the best possible deal for the owner.
   g. To handle all of the paper work as professionally and expeditiously as possible once a sale is made.

3. THE REAL ESTATE OFFICE'S RESPONSIBILITIES:
   a. To support the salesman in his efforts to service the exclusive in every way possible, such as bearing the cost of photographs, signs, newspaper ads, and brochures, if justified.
   b. To maintain a good reputation and an excellent public image so that the maximum number of prospects are attracted: thus there will be a high number of potential buyers for any or all exclusive listings.
   c. To supply the salesmen with all the equipment, auxiliary personnel and general assistance which could reasonably be expected in order to process and consummate a sale. If the three parties uphold their responsibilities, they can hardly miss making a sale.

### The salesman's responsibility
### increases with a short exclusive

Now, in the case of a short-term exclusive, the procedure is slightly different. The responsibilities of the owner and the office remain the same, but the salesman needs to make some adjustments. There is hardly time for newspaper ads or brochures, and catching his co-workers for an inspection on short notice is often impossible. The salesman must now drop everything else and target in solely on finding a buyer for the home on which his exclusive time is limited.

### Use a "crash" program to find a buyer quickly

With me, the first step was usually to go through my prospect index and call everyone that I had worked with for the last six months whom I thought might be interested. Next, I would visit the neighbors on the street to tell them about the house for sale and to ask if they knew anyone in the market for a house. Then I would call all my 'bird-dogs', every restaurant, every motel, every service station, every place of business where I had contacts, and put out a 'bulletin', so to speak, on my latest red-hot listing. Everyone I met would hear about the house, not that I expected them to buy it, but in case they had a relative, a friend, or an acquaintance who was looking for a home, they would learn of my special property.

### Get excited—it attracts attention

All of this has to be done very enthusiastically. If you have enough excitement in your voice as you talk to people, it is infectious. If you make enough calls and contacts enthusiastically, you will be absolutely amazed at the incredible wave of discussion about your listing that will roll through your community in a matter of hours. The odds are about a hundred to one in your favor that your story will reach the ears of someone who is looking for exactly the house you have for sale.

### Sellers are buyers waiting for their home to sell

I had an ace in the hole, also, in promoting this kind of sale. While I waited for my word-of-mouth advertising to spread, I would call the owners of all the houses we had listed. You see, sellers are really buyers waiting for their houses to sell! Somewhere in this group I always found one or more owners eager to inspect my listing. If they wanted to purchase it, a new problem arose because they, of course, had a house to sell, but that could be resolved with the use of contingency clauses, options, delayed closing, trades, or even convincing them to own two homes until I could sell their old one. If this last were the case, I would have another exclusive, and because I had an anxious seller, I had a cooperative one who wouldn't quibble very long over an offer below his price. After all, he wouldn't want to keep two homes any longer than was necessary.

In any event, I found that a crash program to sell a home with a short-term exclusive usually produced a sale. I came to enjoy them: they were a challenge! They whetted my salesmanship, and they made me an awful lot of money.

## SALES THAT SUBSTANTIATE THE VALUE
## OF SHORT-TERM EXCLUSIVES

### The five-day exclusive

Because of my eternal quest for properties to sell, I stopped at a business building where a moving van was moving a tenant. I sought out the owner and asked him for a listing. He would like very much to sell, he said, but was not financially able to let the building stay empty while a buyer was found. He was going to sign a lease with a new tenant on the first of the month, which was five days off. I asked if he would sell if I could find a buyer in five days. He would.

Then I asked if he would give me exclusive rights for those five days. He would, and did.

I was racing with time. I contacted every business for blocks around that I thought could use a building of this size. I spent hours on the phone, racked my brain, and the days went by.

**Sellers are in the classified section; buyers are usually on the front page.** I found my buyer in the "News" section of the newspaper. Scanning the paper at breakfast, I read a report that there had been a fire in a building leased by a bake shop. In short order I was off and running. I located the bake shop owner and was told that he couldn't buy my property, himself, but that if the owner of the burned building would buy it, he would lease it immediately. That was exactly what happened.

An EIGHTEEN HUNDRED DOLLAR commission was earned here because I stopped to check the possibility of a building for sale, and because I was alert to the happenings in the community reported in the newspaper. This was truly putting together a sale, a sale that surely would never have been made if I had not acted on impulse. This is worth remembering.

**Do it now, do it RIGHT NOW!** A real estate man should act the very instant that he sees something or thinks of something that might lead to a sale. If he decides to look into it "this afternoon," or to follow up on it "tomorrow," he will probably never get around to it or, if he does, he will find that some other real estate man who acted on impulse beat him to it. Do it now! Right NOW! That's how you will earn a lot of those additional commissions which will help you sell one million dollars worth of real estate in one year!

### The weekend exclusive

I had received a message from the office secretary to stop at a certain address some time after five o'clock on a Friday evening to discuss with the owners the procedure for selling their home. When I arrived, I was very much impressed with the outside beauty of the home, and the interior was lovely.

**Losing the exclusive doesn't mean the sale is lost.** After a long discussion with the owners covering the steps of marketing their home, I tried desperately to talk them into giving it to me on an exclusive basis for 90 days. They firmly refused. When I proposed 60 days, and then 30 days, they just as adamantly turned me down. They had been instructed by an uncle not to give an exclusive to anyone. I was fighting a lost cause, and I knew it. They were determined to put their house on the open market. I had to figure a way to take advantage of a disadvantage.

Just before I left, they told me that any time after Monday morning I was welcome to show the home. In the meantime, they would be away on a trip over the weekend. A mental bell rang. I saw my chance.

**The important factor of a short exclusive is the head start.** "Since you're going to be gone anyway, will you sign an exclusive with me for two days—Saturday and Sunday? Really, what have you got to lose?"

The suggestion seemed to catch them with their objections down. They agreed, I believe, because they couldn't think of a logical reason not to. I took their key, my 48-hour exclusive, wished them a pleasant trip, and left.

As soon as possible, the next day, I set in motion all the appropriate machinery to promote a quick sale. I made many unproductive phone calls, then finally decided to visit the neighbors.

**If you can get a friend of the buyers to do the selling, it's in the bag.** At the fifth or sixth stop, my sale was made. A young housewife had a friend who was getting married in a few days and was looking for a house. The housewife phoned her while I was there, and did a better job of selling the house than I could have. She was anxious for her friend to live close by, and made an appointment for me for later that evening.

My benefactor and her husband joined us, as well as the family, friends, and relatives of the bride and groom-to-be. They swarmed over and through the house like ants. After a few huddled conferences with various family members, the young couple told me they'd like to buy it.

When the owners came home from their trip, they were greeted by a SOLD sign in their yard. My two-day exclusive had paid off to the tune of ONE THOUSAND SIX HUNDRED FOURTEEN DOLLARS.

### The exclusive "until noon tomorrow"

In every city and community there are a few homes with a distinctive attractiveness all their own, because of a unique architectural design, or a particularly beautiful setting which evokes the admiration of everyone who sees them. Periodically, one of these properties comes up for sale.

**An expensive home that was 100 percent salable.** One morning our office received word that the Lockwood place was going to be put on the market. We were invited to join the other Realtors in town on a tour of inspection the following day at noon. I knew the property—it was a stately English Tudor sitting in the center of magnificent landscaping. I considered it a rare listing, and its salability approached 100 percent. I had no intention of waiting until the following day at noon.

**Negotiating for the right to an advance showing.** Soon I was at the front door, uninvited and a little apprehensive. The owner asked me in, and I came right to the point. I laid my cards on the table: I thought his property was very salable, and there was no doubt in my mind that I could sell it. I was there to ask for the exclusive rights to handle the property.

He would not agree to that, and for nearly an hour I used every technique I knew to try to convince him that it was to his benefit to give me an exclusive. I didn't gain an inch. We chatted a few moments about generalities, and, as I got up to leave, he gave me a smile and a handshake and said,

"I hope to see you tomorrow noon. I'm really sorry I had to disappoint you about the exclusive."

My mind jumped at his words. "Mr. Lockwood, would you do this for me? Would you give me an exclusive on your property until noon tomorrow?"

He thought for a moment and then answered, with a hearty laugh,

"If you believe you can sell my home that fast, I'll give you a chance. I'll give you your exclusive until twelve o'clock tomorrow."

**Twenty-four hours to make the sale.** When I drove away, I was elated. For a little over 24 hours I had the exclusive right to sell one of the finest properties that had ever come on the market in this community. Anyone who thinks selling real estate is dull should experience the blood-racing excitement of such a situation. Waiting somewhere was a buyer for this property, and when I found him I would not only experience the exhilarating satisfaction from a masterful piece of selling, but I would also earn almost THREE THOUSAND DOLLARS in commission.

If I DIDN'T find him, I would be forced to admit failure, and I abhor failure. My audacious contact with the owner had given me a one-day jump on my competitors, so I set out to make good use of that advantage.

**The seven-league advantages of the telephone.** I telephoned everyone I knew, and some I didn't, who might be financially able to purchase this property. I asked each one to give me the names of friends who might be in the market for an outstanding home, assuring them they'd be doing the friend a favor. I called businessmen, city officials, lawyers, doctors and dentists, and they gave me names of friends who might be interested. It made a list long enough to keep me on the phone half the night.

**The search for a buyer circled back to the seller.** One after another my encouraging leads zeroed out. By now it was late, and I decided to call off my search until morning. Then . . . I had an idea. I put in a call to Mr. Lockwood.

"Have you spoken to any of your friends about buying your home?" I asked.

"No," he said, "I would feel a little embarrassed, attempting to peddle my house to my friends."

"Are there any of them in particular who have ever expressed unusual interest in your home?"

"Yes," he replied, "the Grangers—a retired Army officer and his wife, admire our home and have often said they wished they owned one like it."

"Do you mind if I call them?"

"Not at all. Just a minute—I'll give you their number."

How's that for taking candy from a baby?

A little before eleven the following morning, the Grangers bought the Lockwood place. That gave Mr. Lockwood approximately an hour to call the other brokers and cancel the inspection tour.

**Friends of owners are often good prospects.** This profitable transaction could easily have been missed, but I put myself under pressure by taking the short exclusive, which is the greatest value that it has, and by using my brain to explore every possible area where a buyer could be found, even the owner of the house itself.

### Points to remember

1. A short-term exclusive is better than none.
2. When there is limited time, simply accelerate your efforts.
3. There will be a direct lead for the sale of some piece of real estate in the "News" section of tomorrow morning's newspaper.
4. Learn to act on impulse. If you wait to follow up on an idea or a lead *tomorrow,* that's when you will be in the big money —*tomorrow!*

# CHAPTER 21

# MY ANSWER TO A LOADED QUESTION CLINCHED THE LARGEST SALE OF THE YEAR

---

Do you think I can get my price if I wait for another buyer?"

THAT was the question.

Mr. Brooks put his home on the market for a little under $90,000. I brought him a written offer $10,000 below his asking price. Something told me that the purpose for his question lay deeper than idle conversation. He was waiting for my answer.

### The miniature castle in the woods

Mr. and Mrs. Brooks' residence was constructed of cut stone, situated on a small piece of heavily-wooded acreage. It had been built in the 1930's, and age had now softened and beautified it. The numerous windows, seemingly placed at random, were all arched, and small, odd-shaped panes of glass were leaded in place. The roof was slate, the gutters were copper, and the exterior stone walls were nearly covered with clinging vines that had grown even to the top of the high and massive chimney. It was a gray stone mansion with a look of foreverness.

The front entrance was through a heavy, solid oak door which swung on three large, wrought iron hinges. Beyond this opened a wide atrium which, at the far end, led to the foot of a spiral staircase. The four bedrooms on the second level were all spacious, the one on the third floor as large as a dormitory. The huge, high-ceilinged living room, one end of which was all fireplace wall, harked back to the days of King Arthur, with its wide woodwork and corbels of hand-carved natural oak.

**All it lacked was a drawbridge.** There was a sunken dining room overlooking a low-walled patio, from which could be seen a small stream that lost itself among tall hickory trees. Some of the unusual windows, most of the lighting fixtures and the hardware were imported from England. This impressive structure in its lovely natural setting seemed to be straight from an artist's canvas. It is said that a man's home is his castle. In Mr. Brooks' case, his castle was his home.

**There's a buyer for every house even if it's a castle.** Mr. Brooks was willing to part with this property and all its amenities for something near $90,000, and he solicited my help in locating a buyer. I was pleased to have the listing, but more than a little apprehensive about finding a purchaser, since the house was truly one of a kind, foreign to any setting but the English countryside. But there *is* a buyer for every house, and so I took the time to learn everything there was to know about the property in preparation for the day when I would come in contact with a purchaser.

### The four-star production

Fall gave way to winter, and winter to spring, and with the coming of the tulips and lilac blooms came my first opportunity to show the Brooks property. A young executive who had made a meteoric rise to the vice-presidency of his company decided to purchase a home in keeping with his new position. When he described the luxurious appointments he wanted, I'm sure he believed that I had no such property to show him and, indeed, except for the Brooks castle, I didn't.

I felt that I had a rare buyer and a rare house, and that the showing had to be handled with finesse and dramatic artistry. I needed time for the owners to prepare the property, and time for me to rehearse the showing.

My directions were to have the front lawn manicured, the flower beds weeded, the windows sparkling, and a vase of roses in each of the main floor rooms. I wanted the owners to be absent, and, most important, I wanted the sun to be shining. This would all take some doing. I told my prospects that I had a home that would exceed their fondest dreams, but that I needed some time to make arrangements. Then I got busy setting the stage.

Preening the Brooks property took only a couple of days. The weather was bright and clear, and the time had come to show my prospects their new home. With my car freshly washed, I made a trial run from my prospects' home to the front door of the Brooks residence.

**Nothing is so impressive as an attractive entrance.** The timing had to be perfect. I wanted to arrive at precisely one-fifteen in the afternoon, because I had noticed that at that exact same time every day a ray of sunshine broke through an opening in the oak trees and landed squarely on the front entrance, brightening the flagstone approach with its bordering rose bushes, and the single tiny window on each side of the large door. It was like a spotlight, accenting the beauty of the picturesque and friendly entrance.

Remembering the old adage about first impressions, I intended that this should be a somewhat spectacular one, and I wanted everything possible going for me. I was now ready. The stage was set. I left to pick up my audience.

The showing went well. From the time we arrived at the exact minute I had planned, mere words seemed inadequate and superfluous. My prospects inspected the premises slowly but carefully, in nearly silent admiration.

Toward late afternoon, when we settled in the living room, my prospect said,

"I'm utterly amazed that you've brought us to a home that so closely matches what we were looking for. I didn't think it was possible! But this is it, and I'm ready to make an offer."

He named a figure slightly below $80,000, which was approximately $10,000 less than Mr. Brooks was asking. At the office we prepared the purchase agreement; then there was nothing more to do but wait for evening and the return of the owners.

*"I have sold your property," as your opening words, carries great positive impact*

Upon my arrival at the Brooks' residence, timed for after the dinner hour, Mr. Brooks greeted me warmly and took me into the library. He congratulated me on the professional manner in which I had arranged the showing of his property, then seated himself and invited me to do the same. There was a bit of strategy I intended to use, however. I have unfailingly made it a practice to stand when I announce that I have an offer. I often deliberately wait until the owner seats himself to do so. I'm convinced that it gives me a small psychological advantage. It is a little thing, yes—but the fabric of my sales is made from closely-knit little things. And so I remained standing and said to Mr. Brooks,

"I have sold your property—" (with a pause to let that sink in) "provided that the amount of this offer is satisfactory."

Whereupon I handed him a copy of the contract, and sat down.

**Expressing my prejudiced opinions would draw attention to my motives and away from the sale agreement**

Mr. Brooks read every typed and printed word of the purchase agreement with meticulous care. I was suspended in silence, not daring to proceed until he responded. I remained as immobile as the bust of Don Quixote on the mantel, but inside my brain there was a raging desire to speak: to tell Mr. Brooks that it was a good offer, that he probably wouldn't get a better one, and that I thought he should take it. I wanted just to say something, anything before I burst, but I knew that to do so could be fatal.

So I waited, and sweated, and itched, and waited. I had to APPEAR as cool and calm to Mr. Brooks as he did to me, because I knew that he would value and respect an unemotional consideration of the decision before us.

I once read that big decisions are made in silent rooms; therefore, when the silence was broken in *this* room, it was not going to be by me. Finally, Mr. Brooks lowered the document to his lap, and sat momentarily lost in thought. When his words came they were in the form of a question:

**The seller's loaded question**

"Do you think I can get my price if I wait for another buyer?"

Some inner voice told me not to respond too hastily. I didn't know why, then, but I suspected that the deal hung on my answer. Everything I had ever learned about selling real estate directed me to assure him that there was very little chance he would ever get his full price, and that this was probably the best offer he would ever have. This was what all my senses told me to say . . . but I didn't. This was the obvious answer, and the one that he was doubtless expecting.

### If I answered "yes" he might say, "Let's wait."

I reasoned that his motive for asking the question was certainly not to extract the obvious, but at the same time I knew I was risking my deal if I said yes. He was waiting for some response, so I decided to gamble that he had asked me a loaded question:

"Yes, Mr. Brooks, I think you can."

He fumbled in his pocket for a pen, laid the contract on the arm of the chair, and signed it.

### The value was important: the price was not

Mrs. Brooks later told me that if I had answered no, her husband would not have signed the contract. Mr. Brooks was very wealthy, and $10,000 one way or another meant very little to him. It was simply that he wanted me to ADMIT that his house was worth more than the offer I had brought him. It was a display of the eccentricity of the rich.

I had gambled and won, and the winnings were FOUR THOUSAND SIX HUNDRED AND TWENTY DOLLARS.

### Points to remember

1. Expensive homes are not shown impulsively.
2. If the stakes are high, take the time to be perfect.
3. Estate property should be groomed and beautified before being shown to a discriminating buyer.
4. In luxury property, you're selling a way of life: comfort, good taste, and pride of possession.
5. Rehearse your showing, walk through the property alone, spot the highlights you want your prospects to see, and in what order.
6. Wear, mentally at least, a boutonniere, when working with sophisticated prospects.
7. Think for a moment before responding to a question with an obvious answer.

# CHAPTER 22

# HOW I MADE SURE I WOULD BE REMEMBERED

Having business referred to you is a great part of the secret of success. One way to assure referrals is to do an outstanding job of selling, devoting long, hard hours, patience and understanding with people, attention to the little things, and exhibiting a sincere interest in the welfare of buyers as well as sellers. People are anxious and happy to recommend to others those who have served them exceptionally well.

Another way to instigate referrals is to be remembered.

## IF THEY DON'T REMEMBER YOU, HOW CAN THEY CALL YOU?

One of the secrets that I discovered was to make sure of being remembered by the people with whom I came in contact. Today, tomorrow—any day, for that matter—when someone in your community desires the services of a real estate man, the first step they usually take is to reach for the telephone. What a break for you if your name comes to their mind at this moment! One way to work toward this goal is to leave an impression or a reason why they won't forget you, wherever you go.

How to do this can best be demonstrated by explaining the methods I use. My daily activities take me into the homes and businesses of many of the residents of my community. I want them to remember me.

### The cherry pie

When I visit prospects I always deliberately look for something I can admire, compliment them on, or engage them in deep discussion about, to set me apart in their minds from the other real estate people who visit them. I may choose children, pets, pictures, or trophies, as my topic.

In one instance I walked into a lady's house and there, in the center of the kitchen table, was a large cherry pie fresh out of the oven. I made a great to-do about the pie. I told her it reminded me of my grandparents' farm and the cherries I picked for my grandmother to make a pie much like this one. I stated that her husband was a lucky man because women who could bake a cherry pie that looked so good and smelled so delicious were few and far between.

Her smile of appreciation was as glowing as a fire on the hearth. Although I wasn't there on business at this time, you can be sure I told the lady I was in the real estate business.

Over a year later, when these people decided to sell their house, she called my office and said she'd forgotten my name, but she would like to talk to the salesman who liked cherry pie. I got the listing and made the sale, but even before I collected my commission the lady's husband brought me . . . a beautiful cherry pie.

### The trophy

An owner called in various brokers to inspect his property so that he could decide to which of them he would give the exclusive listing. I lingered behind until most of the others had left, and as I wandered about I spotted in the den a tarnished trophy, forlorn and a little dusty. It was almost out of sight, back in the corner of a bookshelf. Upon closer examination, I read the words:

Men's Singles Tennis Champion
Central High School
1927

There was no evidence of other athletic accomplishment anywhere else in the house. I concluded that it was this man's one moment of glory.

A few minutes later I asked the owner about his trophy. It didn't really amount to much, he said, and besides, it was years ago. I wouldn't let him brush it aside. I described how I used to love tennis, had played a little, but was really never very good, although I followed the Wimbledon matches and had always been a great fan of Don Budge's. I assured him I was interested in knowing how he'd won his trophy.

When he sensed my interest was genuine, he gave me a verbal replay of the last two games that won him the championship. I listened intently, congratulated him on his accomplishment and thanked him for telling me about it.

Early the next morning he called the office and asked me to come to his home to discuss the details of an exclusive listing of his property. When I entered the living room, I was warmly pleased to see his now-shining trophy proudly installed on the fireplace mantel.

### The white carpeting

One of the many civic activities I engaged in was the United Community Fund. Making collections one rainy night, I rang the doorbell of the first floor of a duplex. When the lady answered the door, I told her my mission and she invited me in. However, I could see that her living room was covered with beautiful white carpeting so, before entering, I slipped off my shoes, turned them upside down on the stoop and stepped inside in my stocking feet. Nothing was mentioned about this: I completed my business and left.

When the same lady walked in the office a few months later, she looked at the various salesmen; then, pointing to me, she said,

"You're the man I want to talk to. I don't like apartment living. I want my own home again, but this time there'll be no white carpeting."

And she smiled. So did I, because I had hoped she would remember, and was pleased that she did.

### A ten-minute vacation

The opportunity to leave your mark on people doesn't necessarily have to take place in the home. Often when I'm driving and see someone working in the yard, I stop to visit. It is truly wonderful how friendly people can be if you're friendly with them. If their landscaping, or flower gardens, or the home itself is attractive, and you compliment them on it, they will beam. It's the easiest thing in the world to get them to talk about their children, their grandchildren, pets, homes or jobs, where they came from—a multitude of things. It can be a little ten-minute vacation for you, and you can make it a pleasant day for your new-found friends by handing them a compliment or two. Of course, before you leave, tell them you're in the real estate business, and leave your card. Be assured some of them will remember you on some future date when the need for a real estate person arises.

I once gave assistance to a stalled motorist, as I almost always do, only to learn later that the lady was a close relative of a department store executive, who called the office to thank me. My contact with him was directly responsible for a sale that earned me over a THOUSAND DOLLARS in commission.

The object is not only to let people know that you're in the real estate business, but to make them *remember* you as an individual. Passing out business cards is fine—everyone does that—but the idea is to do or say something so out of the ordinary, or so nice, or so unexpected, that you will be remembered, talked about, pointed out, and recognized.

Whoever you are, wherever you go—when you leave, let them know you've been there.


**THINK LITTLE—IT WILL HELP YOU
TO BE REMEMBERED**

Since childhood you have been told to 'think big', but as members of the real estate profession, I say to you, "Think little!" The big things you do by training, and the little things you do because you *think* to do them.

You do the more important things such as keeping an appointment, checking a listing, showing a house, making a closing, drafting a contract, because this is the job you have been trained to do. That's not enough! A real estate man is a composite of a multitude of qualities. Each one that he neglects lowers his stature as well as his income. I maintain that the top man IS the top man because he pays attention religiously to the LITTLE THINGS.

1. He leaves for the office each morning well groomed and well dressed.
2. He has left his personal problems and personal gripes locked in a closet somewhere.
3. He puts a smile on his face, and speaks gently and politely.
4. Throughout the day the key word is courtesy. He opens doors, lights cigarettes, says "Thank you," and "If you please," and "It's been my pleasure."
5. He keeps his car clean and his conversation the same.
6. He is a good listener and a willing advisor.
7. He gives a helping hand, praises his company, and boosts his community.
8. He walks briskly and drives alertly.
9. He attends church, serves on civic projects, and supports charity groups generously.
10. He deals only in facts, and treats all men equally.
11. His appearance, his words, and his actions are always a credit to his profession.
12. He stands proud, he looks successful, he stands out in his community.
13. He is made up of equal parts of knowledge, training, dedication, and compassion, all glued together by a multitude of little things.

I guarantee that it will be greatly to your advantage if you 'Think little'. It just may be what being a real estate person is all about.


## CREATE YOUR OWN PERSONAL TRADEMARK

You can set yourself apart in a variety of ways to help your cause for individuality. Whatever manner you select can become your trademark, so to speak, and will help you to be remembered.

I know a real estate man who wears a miniature rose in his lapel every day. Another man has a two way radio in his car for faster service. (Imagine the effect on a seller if he should call an office to list his home and two minutes later finds a real estate man ringing his doorbell!) Giving a seller an 8 × 10 framed color photograph of his "old" home is the practice of a friend of mine. Another trademark is used by a man who takes a polaroid shot of each home at the time he shows it, and hands it to his prospect to study as they proceed.

Many real estate people drive prestige cars—Cadillacs, Imperials, Mercedes, and so forth, for the purpose of notability. I personally approve of this because I believe a salesman should *look* successful to *be* successful. How confident of the qualifications of a salesman would you be if his degree of success is evidenced by the six or seven-year-old low-priced car that he drives?

### It needn't be spectacular, just unique

One man achieved some renown by being known as the salesman with the alarm wrist watch. You can be sure he arranged for it to "go off" at least once with each new encounter. Large or small, there are many ways to set yourself apart, to be a little more outstanding in order to enhance your chances of being remembered.

My attempt at this has resulted in a closetful of bright-colored sport coats. I have them in fire engine red, gold, powder blue, green, checkered, striped—everything but polka dot.

However, just remember—when you are remembered, then you must produce.

### Points to remember

1. Make your name a household word in your area.
2. Dress well, speak authoritatively, get involved: let the community know you are in the real estate business.
3. Blow your horn long, loud, but melodically.
4. Be wise enough to attend to the little things.
5. Devise your own trademark.

# CHAPTER 23

# HOW INSTANT RECALL LED TO TWO SALES THAT COMPLETED MY MILLION DOLLAR YEAR

—————————

There is one, final, all-important ingredient to add to your plan for success. Without it, I believe it would be impossible to maintain the necessary momentum, day in and day out, to achieve anything like a million dollars of sales in real estate in one year. The best identification I can give it is a REAL ESTATE MEMORY, or REM.

It's hard for me to remember anniversaries, birthdays, and dental appointments. Sometimes I can't think where I've parked my car, but, I can tell you the color and design of the wallpaper in a house I sold eight or ten years ago. Mention a specific or unique feature that you want in a house, and I can tell you where to find it if such a house has ever been on the market in my area.

I can describe in detail what took place during the closing of almost any given sale, and the specific negotiation that brought about the closing. Similarly, I can recall the sales of other real estate people and the step-by-step process they used to make their deals.

*Remember the unusual properties*
*other real estate people usually forget*

I can do this because I cultivated REM. By developing the ability of total recall in matters of real estate, I created an instant inventory. When there was a request for an unusual piece of property it wasn't necessary for me to fumble blindly through the listing book; fake and stall, and finally apologize to my prospects by saying I'd have to look around to see if I could find what they were looking for. Instead, I would draw from my memory bank the exact property I needed, and I usually made my sale.

When there was a particularly puzzling problem, such as matching the buyer with a house, or searching for the elusive reason that prevented a buyer from signing a purchase agreement, I would review the file of previous sales with similar circumstances that I had stored in my memory; then simply apply the methods that had worked before.

### The three parts of REM

1. Vivid and pictorial recall of each and every home that for one or more reasons was different, unique, or outstanding.
2. A mental filing system of uncooperative buyers, problems they presented, and the technique or the peculiar twist of a technique that solved the problem.
3. Storage, for future referral, of the information that other salesmen used to overcome difficulties arising in their sales.

I can't overemphasize the value of developing, to the highest degree possible, a real estate memory. It will assist you in some way in every phase of your real estate career: listing, selling, closing, and building a reputation. It is a powerful tool, without equal.

As I explain REM in more detail, don't forget that in this chapter as, indeed, in the entire book, I am providing you with ways and means to capture sales heretofore lost or not attempted. It is the ADDITIONAL sales throughout the year that are going to put you in the high income bracket. REM is one of the surest ways of doing this.

### Pictorial recall

Anyone who claims that he has a poor memory or lacks the ability of recall simply is not making use of his memory cells. The quality and usefulness of the facts you store in your memory bank must be defined and controlled. The mathematician stores equations, an attorney stores laws because those are the things that are useful and productive in their professions. In your case, pictorial recall of a piece of property will put money in YOUR pocket.

Storing such information requires only that you be alert, observant, and cognizant of features that are unique and unusual. Concentrate momentarily on the feature itself and the location of the property on which it is observed. Get the picture completely and clearly in your mind. Next, associate the property with the owner's name, the address, or a landmark nearby, then deliberately and forcefully place it in your memory. You will be surprised to discover that at the mention of this address, landmark, or distinctive feature weeks, months, or even years later, you will see the entire property in detail in your mind's eye. It will not fail.

### Out-of-the-ordinary properties are sold only by out-of-the-ordinary salesmen

When a prospect with *average* needs contacts an office, the *average* salesman will sell him an *average* house and everyone is happy. The problem is, this salesman remains in the *average* income bracket. The average salesman will miss the additional sales needed to increase his income because, when he is faced with a buyer who requests unique and unusual features, he is lost.

For example, if the buyer is adamant in his demands for a fireplace in a second-story bedroom, a home with a three-car garage, a balcony overlooking the living room, a hilltop location, or any one of a hundred out-of-the-ordinary requests, when the real estate person he's dealing with can only say,

"I'll see if I can locate such a home."

he has lost the buyer. Maybe a year, or even two years ago, he visited a home with a second floor fireplace, but he failed to store that information in his memory bank. THIS real estate man will have to live with an average income.

### If it is a unique property in any manner, REMEMBER IT!

The key word is 'observant'. For instance, let's suppose you are inspecting a home containing extra-wide doors and hallways. Unless you are observant, other features of the house may attract your attention and you may leave the home without even noticing the wide hall and doorways. Now, suppose that a few weeks later you have excellent prospects who have one member of the family confined to a wheelchair. They say to you,

"We hope we don't have to build, but we do need a home with doors and halls that will accommodate a wheelchair."

You have such a home, but due to your lack of observation you don't remember it. No sale. In this example, of course, it's possible that you may have noticed this unusual feature, but paid scant attention, and therefore forgot it. In any event, it culminated unnecessarily in a lost sale.

With practice, pictorial recall CAN be developed by anyone. I'll venture to say that there are homes of friends or relatives which you visited years ago that you can recall vividly today. This memory exists subconsciously. Just think what you could do if you worked at it! I only ask that you give it a fair trial. Through the years it has made me thousands of dollars, and there is no reason why it won't do the same for you.

### Your mental filing system

Each one of us has a mental filing system, even if we aren't aware of it. It is used to store 'mental notes'. We make a 'mental note' to pick up the dry cleaning on our way home, to get the car washed, to write a letter or make a phone call, and we are usually successful in responding to these mental reminders. Now I am going to talk about expanding this mental filing system into a professional, productive, moneymaking part of our makeup.

The need for such a system becomes obvious when a problem arises during a sale. You may remember that the same thing exactly happened before, but you can't remember what you did to solve it. Such situations come in many forms: there may be a buyer with a peculiar personality, or one who reacts abnormally to the usual selling techniques. It could be that the buyers unexplainably put up strong resistance during the very moment of closing: maybe they demand the answer to an out-of-the-ordinary question. Whatever the problem is, the chances are that it has either come up before or will some day come up again.

### Catalogue the answers
### as you do selling techniques

Why fight these battles twice? What worked once will work again, if you can remember what it was. Certainly, no one needs to tell you when you are working with unusual clients, or when you are faced with a unique and puzzling problem: you are well aware of it. Therefore, when you have struggled through the handling of difficult buyers to a successful conclusion, or when you have solved the puzzle or located the key to a problem that was holding up your sale, *remember how you did it.* By that I mean file it in your mental filing system neatly and deliberately, while it's still fresh in your mind, just as you would file a letter in the filing cabinet.

This is done with quiet concentration, just as easily and deliberately as you make a mental note to go by the post office on your way home. By installing a mental filing system, you will save time, wear and tear on your brain and nervous system, and, very possibly, you'll save a sale to add to your year's total that might otherwise have been lost.

Pictorial recall and the mental filing system are STANDARD equipment with all the top producers in the real estate profession.

### Learning from other salesmen

Here is a very useful source of information for our mental filing system. Everyone engaged in selling real estate loves to tell about the 'tough ones' or about a particularly clever bit of selling. When such a story is told, listen carefully, not for entertainment, but as if you were attending a sales seminar. Ask questions if the details aren't clear. If there is something new, a sparkling bit of salesmanship—learn *precisely* how it was done, and file it away. When it is a 'sob story' and the salesman failed to make the sale, try to analyze why he failed. This is an excellent practice in mental gymnastics, and what you think is the solution can be filed away for trial if you should ever be faced with a similar problem. Acquiring these habits comprises a real estate memory as I developed it, and used it. I have saved it for the end of the book because it was responsible for a sizable sale that completed my MILLION DOLLAR YEAR.

*A $27,000 sale that never*
*would have been made without REM*

As I was visiting with friends one evening, a discussion came up about a neighbor across the way. At the conclusion of the conversation my friend, knowing I was interested in houses, asked me if I had ever seen the inside of his neighbor's home. I hadn't, so he proceeded to describe it.

"It's very unusual," he said, "sort of like a mountain lodge— brick floors, inside balconies, mammoth stone fireplace, loft-type bedrooms, and wood-panelled walls."

I like to hear about any unusual property, so I questioned him further. There were a few acres of land, thickly covered with tall pines, and there was a picturesque pond in the back corner of the land. The house was not for sale, and there was nothing to indicate that it would be: however, I mentally filed all this information.

One afternoon almost a year later, a lady seated herself at my desk and proceeded to describe the house she and her husband would like to buy. She wanted a rustic home in a secluded area, with a few acres of land. She wanted lots of wood panelling, a big, old-fashioned fireplace . . . and on and on. A picture of the 'mountain lodge' popped out of my memory bank like toast out of a toaster.

In cases like this, ACTION is the big word. I told the lady I thought I had just the house for her, but first I had to talk to the owner. I prevailed upon her to make herself at home in the office while I drove to the house.

The owner was alone, and when I told him why I was there, he said,

"My wife will probably kill me, but go ahead and show it. I'll sell for $27,000."

Show it I did, and my buyer was overjoyed to find just the house she had described. With the return of the owner's wife, and a fast and furious explanation, that sale was consummated.

**The buyer's emphatic declaration became the guiding clue.** After a cocktail or two to calm themselves, the sellers announced what I already knew—that now *they* needed a home. They described what they wanted, and then went to great lengths to state that there was one area they would absolutely NOT consider. That section of town was OUT, emphatically. I showed them a couple of homes that brought mediocre response, and then I applied the technique described under 'tipoff clues' in Chapter 9: "By telling me what they emphatically WOULD NOT buy, they had told me exactly what they WOULD BUY." I took them to a fine home in the very heart of the area where they said they would not buy, and they bought it. The price was $34,000.

This happened exactly as I have told it. It was a memorable experience in my career. The two sales totalled $61,000, which completed my ONE MILLION DOLLARS worth of real estate in one year.

### Points to remember

1. Use your brain as a photostatic copier to have REM.
2. You normally store mental notes: just expand to include real estate.
3. Why struggle with the same problem twice?
4. Listen and learn from those around you.
5. Never sell property that you wouldn't be willing to buy yourself if the circumstances were the same: this is the Golden Rule of real estate.

# INDEX